Falling Up to Grace

Linda Mabry
1952–2007

Falling Up to Grace

A Memoir

LINDA MABRY

Edited by

Colleen Crangle and David Gleeson

*F*aultline *P*ress
Palo Alto, California

ISBN: 098823520X
ISBN-13: 978-0-9882352-0-5
Library of Congress Control Number: 2012947624

ACKNOWLEDGEMENTS

Shortly before Linda's death, she let her friends Margarita Ramirez and husband, Peadar Dalton, ~~Word did not find any entries for your table of contents.~~ know the status of her memoir that was in progress. She was sad that it would not be completed. In 2005, two years prior to her death, she was chosen to be a resident at Hedgebrook, a retreat for women writers. It was here that she was awarded the prestigious Adrienne Hochstadt Award for her work in progress. Linda was thrilled and surprised to receive this award. It inspired her to continue to write. I wanted to honor her passing by having her memoir published, and many of our friends who read her unfinished draft encouraged me to complete her work. This was, and still is very emotional for me to have gone deep into the heart and soul of my spouse's most personal experiences. Three of my best friends, Joop Verbaken, Stans Kleinjan, and Manon Jannssen never stopped encouraging me, and lifted me up when my own grief and tears were overwhelming. Lastly, I will forever be grateful to Colleen Crangle and David Gleeson. For without their tireless research and hundreds of hours of work this memoir would not exist. Thank you all for making Linda's dream come true.

Dieter Folta
Palo Alto, California

Contents

IN HER WORDS

I first thought about writing this book back in 1999. It is the story of my journey from a quiet corner of Brussels to the projects of East Harlem, a partnership in a prominent corporate law firm, and, ultimately, a professorship at Stanford Law School, and my decision to abandon it all. It is also a story about healing and understanding, about learning to redefine for oneself what it means to be successful.

My story is important not because it is mine but because it is, I think, the story of the daughters of the dream – of the civil rights and feminist movement of the 1960s that enabled women, including some African American women like me, to attain the highest ranks of professions that were formerly the exclusive preserve of white men. Those successes, while still distressingly few, are widely celebrated. What is rarely talked about is the price many of us pay for the privilege of inclusion – the unending struggle to prove ourselves in places where everyone expects us to fail; the requirement that we conform to an ideal that is in many ways antithetical to the essence of our African and feminine beings; the denigration of our inclination to nurture and collaborate as signs of weakness; the unconscious but persistent slights that demean and marginalize us; the loneliness and isolation.

Most of us stay because we worked so hard to get there. We are also not immune to the seduction of money, power, and prestige. We believe we not only have a right but a moral obligation to honor the sacrifices of those who came before and to ease the way for those who will follow. But a growing number of women are walking away from these positions of prestige and accomplishment. Some leave quietly. Some choose to remain unemployed. Others choose to work in jobs with responsibilities and pay far below their levels of education and experience. All are struggling to redefine what it means to be successful.

In this book, my travails at Stanford University, at the height of my profession, form a pivot for my reflections on my American journey and on race and gender in the United States at the dawn of the new millennium. I want this to be an eloquent, brutally honest account of the emotional trauma of racism and sexism, but also the story of my odyssey toward healing and understanding.

Linda Mabry
January 2004, Palo Alto, California

Linda accepting Hochstadt Prize for work-in-progress, *Falling Up To Grace*, at Hedgebrook Writers in Residence, 2005.

Childhood: Hope and Ambition

"And this is for colored girls who have considered suicide / but are movin' to the ends of their own rainbows."

Ntozake Shange -
For Colored Girls Who Considered Suicide When the Rainbow is Enuf

DOES THE BLACK RUB OFF?

✤

IN MID-TWENTIETH CENTURY America, my father had to go abroad to get the sort of medical school education that was out of reach to a poor black boy from Georgia. He'd worked for several years at the Brooklyn Navy Yard after graduating from City College of New York, and wasn't surprised when Columbia University turned him down for medical school, but he was outraged when Howard University did, too. So he started looking at schools abroad. The moment the *Université Libre de Bruxelles*[1] offered him a spot we gave up our apartment, sold all our possessions, and, in August 1955, boarded a Dutch ship bound for Rotterdam.

1955 Linda and Tommy, ready to disembark from Dutch passenger ship "Zuiderkruis" (Southern Cross) as it docks in Rotterdam, Holland.

We arrived in Belgium in September 1955, on the eve of one of the coldest, fiercest winters on record.

Our first home was at the back of a tenement building on *Rue des Tanneurs*, a narrow medieval street in the center of Brussels. It had two dark, dank rooms, one leading straight into another.

The immediate neighbors were mostly kind and accepting. We had poverty in common, poverty that defined our lives. They admired my father's courage and determination. He reminded them of the brave American Negro soldiers who'd helped liberate Europe from the scourge of the Nazis. And they could empathize with my mother's visible pregnancy. It evoked hope in the midst of bleakness and drew them to us.

Soon after we moved in, an old woman from the one-room flat across the way brought an offering of food: a small roasted bird of some kind. After thanking her, my mother took the plate, shut the door, rushed to the sink – the lone source of water in our flat – and heaved. Later, when the same neighbor invited us over, we didn't tell her we hadn't eaten the bird. Between sips of bitter coffee and tales of wartime hardships she showed my mother how to twist sheets of newspaper into tight strands to help fuel a coal stove. *"C'est ce qu'on a fait pendant la guerre."* That's what we did during the war, she said. But the tiny amount of heat radiated from burning paper was never enough to conquer the cold and damp.

One day the couple downstairs offered to watch Tommy and me while my mother went to market. The wife had waist length black hair, long thin fingers, a long thin nose, and a long thin body wrapped in a blood red robe. To me she looked just like a witch. I insisted I didn't want to stay with her, but my mother said I had to. "Tommy is with you," she told me. "Be a good girl. I won't be long." So I sat at the witch's table, turning pages of *Snow White*, thinking, I'll be okay as long as she doesn't try to touch me.

It turned out I was wrong. It wasn't the witch we should have feared so much as her husband. One bitterly cold morning, he knocked on our door offering to pick up coal for us. Given the streets outside were thick with snow, my mother gratefully accepted, handing him 10 Francs and expecting him back within the hour. But he didn't return until late afternoon, and when he did he was empty handed – no coal, no Francs. He claimed he'd lost our money.

Of course, this petty theft could have happened to anyone, and probably did – even within the same building. In that sense we were all in the same boat but other incidents made me aware that we were different, other, apart.

Dressed up in our Sunday best, my mother, my father, my brother, Tommy, and I were out for a stroll. As we made our way down the streets of our new city, I stopped and pressed my face against giant plate glass windows of shops we passed – fascinated more by my the marks my breath made than the displays. Instead of walking a straight line I skipped around in circles, hearing but not heeding my mother's gentle admonition about falling too far behind. When we passed the recessed entrance of a small apartment building, I ducked inside, drawn by a shiny panel of buzzers and nameplates. I stood there staring up at this temptation, feeling mischievous yet not quite bold enough to press one of the buzzers. When I finally tore myself away and headed back to the street, my parents and brother had vanished. Feelings of surprise and disbelief soon gave way to panic and despair.

I stood in the middle of the sidewalk, cheeks streaked with tears, unable to move or speak. Around me a crowd of onlookers had gathered, staring. Beyond my fear of being lost and separated from my mother, I sensed something more was going on. Their looks were not so much concern for a lost child, as curiosity over this strange little being in front of them.

At some point a woman stepped forward and spoke. Her voice sounded kind but the strange words she spoke held no meaning for me.

Eventually my mother came back and grasped my hand and pulled as the gawking strangers stood aside to let us pass. "I told you to keep up," she said – her voice mixed with displeasure, fear, and love.

Then came another day when we weren't so much strolling as purposefully headed for a destination. This time it was only the three of us, without my father. I stayed close to my mother, never letting her out of my sight. As we made our way across a traffic circle, I became aware of cars and pedestrians that should have been moving but instead they had come to a complete standstill. Eyes were fixed upon us, full of surprise; fingers pointed at us; people in pairs or groups exchanged animated whispers. I couldn't understand their foreign words, but I knew they were talking about us. As we hurried away the warmth of my mother's palm in mine was reassuring, but her quickening pace was not. Nor was the urgency in her voice: "Do *not* let go of my hand."

Safely home that evening, my father told us, "People here have never seen Negroes." It couldn't have been first time I'd heard the word "Negro," and I must have known I was a Negro, but until then I hadn't known what it meant. In that moment I knew: It meant that people would stop, stare, and point at you in the street.

Another time the three of us were out, a woman walked up to my mother who was holding Tommy and me firmly by the hand. The woman smiled, spoke some gentle words, and looked down at me with sympathetic eyes – then she swiped my cheek with her bare hand. My mother pulled me away so abruptly I almost lost my balance. "Don't you touch my child!" she said. The woman stepped aside, a look of feigned incomprehension on her face. We sped down that street so fast my feet were a blur. When we reached the corner and stopped before crossing, I looked back to see the woman examining her upturned hand, as if she were looking for traces of my brown face on her palm.

Later that evening, Tommy and I were in bed in the back room. I heard my parents talking as they emptied the warm, gray soapy water from the metal tub in which they had just bathed us. "That woman put her filthy hands on my child's face – trying to see if the black would rub off," my mother said, indignantly. "Never in my life have I seen such ignorant people."

"She didn't mean any harm," my father replied. "They've never seen brown skin before. They've never seen anything so beautiful."

I wondered. My father says Negroes are beautiful. I know that beautiful is a good thing to be. People always smile when they tell me I'm beautiful, and they say it with affection. But I'm not sure being a Negro is a good thing. I want to be beautiful but I'm not sure I want to be a Negro. I don't want to be anybody's curiosity.

Tommy and I were enrolled in the local *jardin d'enfants* [nursery school]. As if by magic, we began to understand the language of the children and teachers around us.

Outings alone with my father were rare, cherished events. My very first time at the movies, he took Tommy and me to see *Lady and the Tramp*. I felt small but important standing beside him, beneath a giant marquee emblazoned with thousands of tiny lights. I felt the same way sitting at his side in the vast darkness of the theater. When the curtain drew and the screen lit up, I moved to the edge of my red velveteen seat, just to be closer to the magic.

I became enthralled by Lady's life: the sumptuous grandeur of her house; the loving attention her owners lavished upon her; her jeweled neck and languid, innocent eyes; her long ears that framed her face like a mane of red hair; her happy carefree, existence. But I was also drawn to Tramp – a ruggedly handsome, fiercely independent, smooth talking, street-smart, man-about-town. Shot at by chicken farmers, hunted by the evil dogcatcher, and chased down filthy alleys by bands of vicious dogs, his existence was far more precarious than Lady's, and yet he exuded self-confidence and a *joie de vivre*. I wanted both the luxuriant comfort of Lady's life and the wild excitement of Tramp's. A similar tension would come to rule many of my adult years.

Two scenes from *Lady and the Tramp* left such an impression on me that nearly fifty years later I can still close my eyes and see them as clearly as if I were beside my father in that darkened theater.

The first scene was Lady and Tramp's night out on the town – their spaghetti dinner so daintily consumed, one long, sensuous noodle at a time, followed by a midnight stroll through moonlit hills, serenaded by melodious voices coming from the sky, singing *Bella Notte*. I was transported by that utterly perfect moment. In the years to come it would infuse me with a comforting, joyful nostalgia whenever I thought of it – as I would over and over again.

In the second scene, while chasing the dogcatcher's coach, Trusty was crushed under the coach's wheels. That screen moment touched a sadness in my core I hadn't known existed. Whether it was the tragic end to a story that only moments before had filled me with such hope and joy, or empathy for what I was sure had been such a painful end to a gentle dog's life, I cried so much I missed most of the rest of the movie. I barely even noticed the happy ending in which everyone, including old Trusty who had survived the coach accident with his bandaged foot, reunites at Lady's House.

"See. Trusty's fine," my father said as he moved me to his lap. "He just hurt his foot a little. They're all going to live happily ever after."

"Are you sure he's alright, Daddy? Are you sure? I saw him get crushed by the wagon wheels!"

"Trusty's gonna be just fine. Really, he is."

I asked my father for reassurance about Trusty's fate again and again that afternoon, and throughout the evening, and into the days that followed. I was never quite convinced by his patient explanations. I suspected he was just telling me those things so I'd go to sleep without crying. Such reassurances became fewer and farther between in the years to come.

In February 1956 I gained a new sister, Margueritte. 'Maggie' wasn't chocolate brown like the rest of us, but the color of golden sand.

Because he was a medical student, my father had been invited to attend Maggie's birth. Later, he told my mother how the doctors had looked at him incredulously when Maggie first appeared. "*Vous êtes content, monsieur?*" one of them asked.

My father said, "The doctor's head was spinning round the room. He looked at Maggie's fair skin, then at your ebony face, then at my brown skin, then at the baby again, just trying to make sense of it all." The doctor's look and tone conveyed a question he dared not speak: 'How can you be happy, *monsieur*? This child couldn't possibly be yours!' My parents both laughed. "They don't know our babies are born light and get darker with time." I wondered, is it possible that Maggie is not a Negro? But how could she *not* be when she came from inside my mother?

Above the basinet in my mother's hospital room where Maggie lay swaddled in blankets, was a sign. It had a drawing of a patch of colorful cabbages with pink babies resting in some of them, and words written below. My father told me they said, "*Regardez moi, mais ne me touchez pas!*" Look, but don't touch! I wondered, *is that sign so they won't try to rub the color off her face?*

CHAUSSÉE DE BRUXELLES

✤

*"**R**ue des Tanneurs, cela n'est pas pour vous, monsieur."* It's not for you, sir, the university officials told my father, suggesting he might want to move his family to a "better" neighborhood.

Once the snow had thawed and spring flowers began to push through, we moved to a wide, quiet, residential street full of sunshine and light named *Chaussée de Bruxelles*.

Our home was a four-room flat on the top floor of a three-story residence. Two connecting rooms divided by a pocket door ran the length of the flat. The front room, overlooking the street, was where we all slept – Maggie in her crib, Tommy and I in bunk beds, my mother and father in a double bed. The back room, overlooking the garden, was where we gathered for meals and homework and play, and entertained the occasional visitor. Adjacent to the back room was a small kitchen with a balcony overlooking the garden. The best thing about our new place was that we no longer had to share a toilet. We had our own water closet in one corner of the kitchen. Also, we no longer had to bathe in a gray metal tub filled with water heated on the coal stove. Instead, we had a white ceramic tub with a coin-operated water heater.

The apartment even had a small study for my father. It smelled of formaldehyde, seeping from under the lid of a bucket that held the human brain my father dissected, guided by his anatomy book. There was also a collection of miscellaneous stale smelling human bones, including a femur and skull.

The owners of the building, Monsieur and Madame Ouasson, lived on the first floor. They were missionaries just back from the Congo. To me, they were fat and old. To them, we looked just like the people whose souls they went to save. They treated us affectionately, but with condescension – allowing us to sit in their garden on Sundays.

Summer came, and my father went back to America to work on a construction project, helping build an Interstate Expressway[ii]. He returned with a brown baby doll for me. She was beautiful. I held her gently in my arms as I sat on my father's lap. I loved him. I'd missed him, and I was happy he was home.

Tommy and I were enrolled in a new school a few blocks from our new home. I was in first grade, he was in second. It was there that I learned to write. I loved the order and precision that governed the writing ritual. It made life feel certain and predictable. We wrote on paper where each line was subdivided into five smaller ones – like musical staves. We were instructed to fit our letters precisely into the allotted spaces: lower case between the first two lines, and tall letters like "t" reaching up to the second line. Capital letters were formed with a precisely defined flourish of loops and swirls, and extended up to the third line. When you wrote, you were to tilt your notebook slightly to the left so that your writing angled gently. We wrote with *porte-plumes*, colorful wooden pens with shiny brass or silver nibs. The thick base of mine felt just right when grasped between my fingers. If I dipped the nib into the inkwell just right, covering it with just the right amount of ink, and holding the pen at just the right angle with just the right amount of pressure, it would glide across the page allowing me form perfect letters within their allotted spaces.

I remember the teacher strolling up and down the aisles of wooden desks monitoring our progress. She paused upon reaching mine. *"Très bien. Très bien ma petite."* You see, I said to myself, if you follow the rules the results will be beautiful and satisfying, and you will be praised. Only as my career progressed would I learn how wrong an assumption this could be.

One beautiful spring day, a truck hit a little boy from my school. I can't remember if he was in my class or if I even knew him. I seem to recall he lived near us, maybe even on the same street. I didn't see the accident but I remember being told that the truck's wheels ran over his head and crushed it.

"Will they fix him like they fixed Trusty?" I asked my mother, still anxious from *Lady and the Tramp*.

"He's dead, and can't be fixed. That's what happens when children don't listen – and that's why I tell you every day to be careful crossing the street."

I wasn't sure I knew what "dead" meant. I knew the words of the children's evening prayer I had recited every night since I was old enough to speak... *If I should die before I wake, I pray the Lord my soul to take.* I guessed death must be like a sleep from which you don't wake up.

What haunted me was not the young boy's death but the manner of it. My mind conjured up a scene so real it was as though I'd been an eyewitness; forcing me to watch it a hundred times a day. A small, slender, happy boy runs into the street, satchel in hand. He never sees the truck that strikes him, dragging his head under its giant wheels. All that's left is a bloody, fair-haired pancake atop an intact body lying in the middle of the boulevard. If I don't want to die like that boy, I thought, I'd better listen up to my mother. The lesson must have stuck. In more than 50 years, I can't recall a single time I disobeyed her.

Soon, I had a new friend who lived down the street. My mother gave me permission to go to her house and play. Her mother admired my hair and asked me how I got it to look so pretty. I told her about using a hot comb and pressing. Next time she saw my mother, she asked her about this. When I came home from school, my mother yelled, "*Never, ever* tell anyone how I do your hair!" Her voice was loud and harsh. "I don't want these people in my business!"

Getting my hair pressed was an elaborate, time-consuming, and often painful production. But I didn't know it was supposed to be a secret. It happened once or twice a month when my hair was washed. My mother would sit in a chair by the stove while I'd sit between her legs, perched on a stack of my father's medical textbooks. Washing had turned my hair into a tangled, nappy mess. Taming it required combing out the knots – a process that left my scalp sore for days on end – and then pressing the untangled strands with a short-toothed metal comb that had been heated on the stove. Starting at the front, my mother would methodically part my hair into two inch segments, slather each thick wooly strand with special hair grease sent from America, then iron it straight by running the hot comb through. The grease melted and sizzled in the comb's wake, sometimes searing me as it oozed onto my head or down the nape of my neck. Sometimes my scalp was scorched if she held the comb too close to the roots. Sometimes, her hands were oily and the comb would slip, bumping against my earlobe where it would leave a serrated burn mark.

Maybe I wasn't supposed to tell anyone how my mother pressed my hair in case they might think she didn't love me the way she should? I might have yelped and grimaced through those hour-long sessions, which felt like they lasted the better part of a day, but I would always sit perfectly still and never cried. To keep me from getting restless or focusing on the discomfort and occasional pain, she would tell me stories about America and her Alabama girlhood. I relished the physical closeness to my mother, especially being the sole object of her attention. It told me with an unshakeable certainty that I was loved.

There were three other Negroes in Belgium that we knew: Nat, Eddie, and Aunt Hazel. On the rare occasions we would pass a brown man on the street Maggie always cried after them –"*Papa! Voilà Papa!*"

Nat and Eddie were two medical students at the university in Louvain. When they came to visit us we sat in the back room overlooking the garden. Eddie did magic tricks – like making coins disappear from one hand and reappear in the other, or making my mother's hairpin appear at the bottom of a closed jar of Vaseline. The house was full of laughter when they visited. We'd beg for one more magic trick before we were sent off to bed, long past our usual bedtime. They talked with my parents late into the night. Not wanting the day to end, I lay in the bottom bunk in the next room, feeling safe in the warmth and softness of my flannel pajamas with the added protection of thick wool blankets. I fought in vain against sleep as it overcame my efforts to eavesdrop on their conversation.

Then there was Aunt Hazel, a fellow student with my father at the *Université Libre de Bruxelles* School of Medicine. Her face was large, as were most of its features – a full nose, spacious eyes, and big teeth – only her lips were thin. She had a full bosom and hips to match. Her hands were broad and thick but also warm and reassuring.

Her home was a collection of small rooms, two floors up in a low-rise tenement building. The furniture was drab and sparse but the place felt crowded nonetheless. In the corner of one room was a shelf lined with jars of fetuses she'd brought home from the lab.

At her place, a large pot was always slow cooking on the stove. Anything that had to do with food, Hazel did slowly. She took longer than anyone I have ever known to work her way through a plate of food.

Aunt Hazel had a daughter named Lilly but she didn't have a man. I once spent a weekend with them. We went to a small amusement park where I rode around in the toy train a dozen times at least, able to extend my stay because I kept catching the tassel at the end of the large ball the attendant controlled from a cord in his booth. I could see Aunt Hazel and Lilly shouting at me but I couldn't hear their words above the din of the ride. Later, I learned they were trying to tell me not to catch the tassel because it was time to go home. The attendant had apparently been deliberately allowing me to catch it. I think I may have been the only child on the ride that night, and I felt so special. In my large family, it was unusual to be noticed, let alone be the center of attention.

We found each other again when we all returned to Harlem in the early 1960s. Hazel lived in another dark low-rise tenement while completing her internship and studying for the foreign medical graduate's exam.

When she finally got her license, she went into practice with my dad for a while. But that didn't work out. He was highly critical of her. He thought she was too timid. She ended up taking a "job" at a hospital – a move my father regarded as emblematic of defeat. To him, working for anyone other than yourself was the worst thing you could do. In later life, I wondered if Aunt Hazel could ever have done anything right in my father's eyes. More so when he himself ended up working for a large, impersonal corporation.

Almost all the time we spent with Hazel in those Harlem days centered on meals – in particular Sundays and holiday dinners. My brothers and sister and I were always thrilled to see her, not least because she always brought a purse full Wrigley's spearmint gum and gave us each a stick to chew. She also brought laughter and levity to a dinner table all too often dominated by my father's ominous soliloquies.

Eventually, Hazel did well enough to buy a condo in a high-rise building at 140th Street and Lenox, a mink coat, and a yellow Cadillac that she never learned to drive. But that was small in terms of the significance of her achievements. At age 40, in an era when few women had career aspirations, this black woman had left an abusive husband, moved to Europe as the single mother of an adopted child, and put herself through medical school.

PLACE DE LA RÉSISTANCE

❧

LATER WE MOVED to *Anderlecht*, a Flemish neighborhood on the outskirts of the city. All six of us were crammed into three small rooms on the northern edge of a large, tree-lined square. Our 'apartment', at number 19, consisted of a kitchen at the rear with a coal stove for cooking and a window ledge that served as a refrigerator; a windowless middle room which my parents claimed as their own – even though you had to traverse it to get to the other two; and finally, a front room which doubled as a bedroom for the children and a living room for the whole family – it had a coal stove for heating, and a large bay window looking out over the square. Up a narrow flight of stairs from the kitchen was a tiny half bath with sink and toilet. One flight down was a tub room we shared with the building's other tenants. Two flights down and you were on the street facing the square that was the center of my life: *Place de la Résistance.*

Place de la Résistance, Brussels

An unremarkable square, its outermost border was lined with oak trees. Leaves defined the seasons which otherwise would be indistinguishable in cold, gray, wet weather that persisted throughout much of the year. Between this outer ring and the paved interior lay a stretch of sand-colored dirt and gravel. On the edge sat wrought iron and wooden benches that would quickly fill on sunny days, or when withered old men wearing caps and worn jackets would gather to play "*balle pelote*" – a game whose rules and object I never knew, but it involved rolling hard, fist-sized balls on the ground toward other stationary balls. The center of the square was unadorned – no fountain, no statue – just an expanse of concrete perfect for playing hopscotch, jumping rope, or just running wild.

Some of the buildings around the square, including ours, had small businesses on the ground floor – a hairdresser, a dry cleaner, and several bars with outdoor cafés; a small grocery; and a take-way restaurant. Our favorite place was the restaurant. Whenever there was a little extra cash at home my brothers and sister and I would get 5 Francs to buy a pile of "*frites*" – what Americans call "French fries." We peered up at the counter as the fries were handed down to us wrapped in paper. If we could scare up an extra Franc, or sometimes even if we couldn't, the *frites* would also be drenched in mayonnaise. We'd haul the whole salty, greasy package across to the square and sit on benches, oblivious to our surroundings until the last *frite* had been consumed.

Justice de Paix, Brussels

An imposing redbrick *Justice de Paix* [courts of justice type building] dominated Place de la Résistance. Its enormous lead glass windows overlooked the square like the watchful eyes of a god. Other buildings bordering the square were mostly turn of the century residential structures, two to four stories high. These narrow brick and stone buildings had tall windows, some of which were adorned with decorative arches or medallions. Most had a single narrow terrace with a wrought iron railing at the center of the upper floors. Some of the larger buildings may at one time have been single-family homes for wealthy merchants, but by the 1950s they had all been carved up into tiny, working class apartments.

Number 19, the building that contained our apartment, stood almost in the center of the square's northern border and housed the dry cleaner. I must have crossed that square a thousand times as I made my way about the neighborhood: on my way to the tram that carried us to school; or to the bakery around the corner for bread and sometimes cakes; or to the Saturday afternoon cinema for a Tarzan movie with scenes of man-eating black savages that caused other children to look at us nervously when the house lights came up at the end of the show.

I danced around that square all alone in the rain one afternoon until my mother called me home, and, even though I was drenched, she didn't scold me because I think she saw my joy. On more than one occasion, I stared down into that square from our bay window, sitting on the edge of a chair, elbows leaning on the sill, looking for comfort in the familiar.

Place de la Résistance was my anchor. In the confusion of our precarious expatriate life it tied me securely to an identifiable, manageable space. Even though as a child I experienced it as a safe haven, the name always conjured up images of a bloody but heroic uprising, like the one so vividly described in the *Marseillaise* – the French national anthem we were required to memorize at the Lycée. Today, I can't help but wonder if that vision had somehow been prescient. The streets of Harlem we would make our next home in turned out to be a real live battlefield, full of blood but short on heroes.

The heart of our house on Place de la Résistance was the kitchen, and the heart of the kitchen was a long wooden table at its center.

Every morning we gathered around that table, pulling our well-worn sweaters tight to ward off the chill the coal stove had yet to dissipate. The table would be set with mix-and-match mugs of steaming hot chocolate and mix-and-match plates on which to rest the thick slices of bread we slathered with butter and jam or topped with slices of cheese, or on occasion, with mix-and-match bowls of hot oatmeal made from Quaker Oats sent from America.

It didn't take us long to get to table after Mom had roused us from our bunks. We'd clamber up the back stairs, into the small half-bath for a quick swipe with a washcloth lathered in soap and cold water, then we'd scurry back down to 'our room' to slip into clean underwear. Maybe we'd have a freshly laundered shirt or blouse to go with yesterday's pants and skirt – the same hand-me down pants and skirt we'd get to wear to school every day, week in, week out.

We ate quickly, usually in silence, then we'd head out across the square to catch a 56 tram bound for Gare du Midi – a short walk from the Boulevard Poincaré and its venerable *Lycée Français de Bruxelles*.

Every school day afternoon Tommy, Maggie, and I would huddle around that table under my mother's watchful, hopeful, weary eyes. My baby brother, Jerry, wailed from his high chair – placed a safe distance from the temptations spread out upon our learning platform.

"*Lis cette phrase une deuxième fois* – and do it right this time," my mother admonished Maggie with loving sternness as she stirred a pot of leek soup on the stove.

"*Pa-pa a ta-pé To-to,*" Maggie said as she dragged her pudgy index finger with deliberation across the page.

"*Papa a tapé Toto. Papa a tapé Toto. Toto a tapé Pape!*" Tommy and I echoed mockingly, laughing too loud at our perversion of the phrase that had the little boy Toto striking his father.

"*Arrête!*" my mother warned. We stopped laughing and lowered our heads till our noses were practically touching the pages of our workbooks, unsure whether she was admonishing us for making fun of Maggie or for disrespecting our quick-to-use-the-strap father.

"Linda Ann!" my mother shouted.

I knew I was in trouble when she used my middle name.

"*Cinq fois sept* is what?" Mom said, exaggerating her incredulity as she pointed to my calculations in pencil.

"*Trente ... Oh! Non! Trente-cinq, excusez moi.*"

"*Fais attention à ton travail ma fille.*"

My arithmetic may have been careless, but never my penmanship.

Clockwise from top: Tommy, Linda, baby Jerry, and Maggie

When schoolwork was completed to mother's satisfaction, my siblings and I would clear the table and set down four soup bowls or supper plates – one for Tommy, one for Maggie, one for Mom, and one for me. Jerry ate in his high chair. And Dad, who studied late into the night at the university rarely made it home in time to eat supper with the family.

It was at that table I learned to love learning. It was also at that table I learned to fear hunger. A fear I would learn to master in just one, unforgettable day.

Outside was still light, so it must have been a summer afternoon when we'd have been having an early supper. I can see my mother standing at the coal stove making eggs and rice. She's melting a spoonful of butter in a frying pan, pouring in a large bowl of left-over boiled rice, and whisking together all the eggs she has, which, as usual, amounts to fewer than the number of mouths gathered around the table.

Eggs and rice was my father's specialty. It's the only dish I've ever known him to make and he usually did so with great fanfare. Somehow it always tasted less special when my mother made it and watching her do it was not nearly as enthralling.

Tommy, Maggie and I were seated at the table, fidgeting and making a racket as my mother dished spoonfuls of rice onto our plates. She must have shouted because we heard her words clearly above our clamor.

"You kids had better be quiet and eat. This is the last of the food we've got, and I don't know where our next meal is coming from."

The room grew as silent as if we'd all dropped dead. You couldn't even hear our breathing.

Not a single grain of rice remained on my plate that afternoon. And ever since that day, whenever food is present I cannot pass it up. I'm driven to eat all I can by the quiet, urgent whisper of a girl child I cannot see. *"You never know,"* she warns me, *"Tomorrow, there may be nothing to eat."*

Food scarcity was not the only threat we faced. My earliest memory of Tommy getting beaten was a rare sunny day. The bay windows facing the plaza were flung wide. Maggie, Tommy, and I were going out to play. As we launched down the stairwell heading for the streets, Mom reminded Tommy to look after his "baby sister." I don't know how it all came together but I can still see the moment as if it were a freeze frame – projected onto a big screen before an empty theater. On the east side of the plaza, Maggie is standing between trolley tracks that run down the middle of the street. The front end of a trolley car is just inches from her face. People in the plaza, on the streets, and in the trolley car remain frozen: their bodies paused, mid-motion; mouths agape, speechless; eyes wide with surprise and fear. Mom is leaning from the bay window, arms extended towards her baby daughter, moving with a vigor that suggests she's trying to reach out across the plaza and snatch her child from the tracks.

In the next frame the tracks are clear, the trolley and the people have started to move on. Only I'm still frozen in place. Maggie and Tommy are back inside, upstairs with our father and mother. I stand in the middle of the plaza, gazing up at the open bay window, my head tilted to capture the sound of belt hitting flesh, my father's rage, and my brother's screams.

I guess Dad must have thought he could beat Tommy straight whenever Tommy veered off the path Dad had in mind. But I think it had the opposite effect. The beatings and the rage threw Tommy completely off course. Today, at 53, he's more lost than ever. No one in the family, not even his own children, knows where he is.

BEST FRIENDS

❦

DESPITE BEING POOR, I never recall feeling deprived except for the subtle nagging worry we might run out of food. That was because, for the most part, we socialized within our means – my parents' friends and the children we played with were generally as poor as us. The one exception was my friend Marie Christine.

Marie Christine and I were classmates at the Lycée. I don't recall how we came to be best friends. But I do know that she was the only one of my classmates ever to invite me home. I hadn't realized until recently that the vast majority of students at the Lycée were rather well-to-do children of diplomats, international bankers, and the like. Perhaps that's why they didn't invite me home. But Marie Christine was different. She was an orphan who'd been adopted by a wealthy, older woman from the Hanlet family – venerable Belgium piano makers and sellers. They lived in an apartment above the *Maison Hanlet* on *Rue Livorne* – with its expansive showroom offering scores of Hanlets, Steinways and other fine pianos for sale. When I visited her we often played hide and seek in the showroom making our way around the pianos as if they were trees in a dense forest.

Although I considered Marie Christine my best friend, I don't know if she ever thought of me in the same way. I always sensed that her mother, a warm and generous woman who invited me to call her Tante Agnou, had encouraged our friendship.

One day in the schoolyard at recess I overheard a group of girls talking about what gifts they planned to take to Paule Micheaux's birthday party. I hadn't known Paule had a birthday coming up or even that she was having a party. There was no reason I should have known – Paule and I were not especially close. We sometimes played together in the groups of half a dozen or so children that came together spontaneously at recess, but we wouldn't have sought each other out individually. That said, I didn't think the other girls were any closer to Paule than me, so I was deeply disappointed when I learned they'd been invited and I hadn't.

1962 – Lycée Français, Brussels – 5ᵐᵉ Anée.

My life in working-class Anderlecht and my life at the venerable Lycée Français on Boulevard Poincaré were so separate that until that day I hadn't even realized classmates could be playmates outside school. I had never been to any of my classmate's homes, nor had they been to mine. If there was a network of relationships beyond the schoolyard, I wanted to be part of it.

So I decided to try and get myself invited to the party by giving Paule a present. I hoped it would make her feel like she had overlooked a friend, a mistake she would surely seek to correct by extending me a belated invitation. Buying a gift was out of the question. I had no money of my own and knew my parents didn't have any to spare for such frivolities. Instead, I decided to give Paule a book that had recently been given to me.

I don't remember the title of the book but I do remember exactly what it looked like. It was a hardback with a grass green spine and a sunshine yellow cover embossed with golden *fleur-de-lis*. Nor can I remember what the book was about. I have a vague recollection it was a fantasy story for little girls. I know I'd read it multiple times but can't be sure if I did so because I was enthralled by the story or by the fact that it had been given to me – and *only* me – by a cherished family friend when it wasn't even Christmastime or my birthday. Presents were a rarity outside of holidays and birthdays. When we were given one, it was usually a collective gift intended for my three siblings and me to share equally. The book looked as if it had been read a few times but that didn't concern me. I convinced myself Paule would be so moved by my unexpected kindness she wouldn't notice.

When I told my mother I wanted to make a present of my book and asked her if she would help me gift-wrap it, she seemed puzzled.

"I know how much this book means to you," she said. "So why would you want to give it to a girl you've never even mentioned before?"

The gift-wrap and ribbon we used were also secondhand, but I didn't care about that either. My carefully thought out plan was about to be realized and I was giddy with excitement.

In the morning I headed for the tram on the way to school with a sense of embarking on an important mission. Boarding was awkward because I had to hold the present in one hand and my heavy book bag in the other. I usually tried to avoid doing anything that might draw attention to myself because I was mortified by the gapes my brown skin so often provoked. It would've been easier to climb those high steps on the tram if I'd put the present in my schoolbag, but I wanted to keep it constantly in sight to ensure it didn't get damaged or lost.

Arriving at school, I went straight into the classroom ahead of the other students, placed the gift inside my desk, and sat through the rest of the morning, inattentive to my lessons, anxious only for the recess bell. When it rang, I waited for the classroom to empty before retrieving my precious package and heading into the schoolyard. Instead of immediately running into the center of the yard as was my custom, I slipped behind one of the thick pillars lining its edges, keeping the book hidden behind my back. As soon as I spotted Paule, I ran out and handed her my gift.

"*Bon anniversaire, Paule!*" I said too loudly. Paule, immaculate and prim as ever, smiled graciously as her light blue eyes radiated confidence. "*Merci,*" she said in her soft voice. I turned and ran, not wanting to betray how much I had invested in that moment.

Next day, Paule's mother called my mother to ask if I'd come to the party. They spoke in English – a seemingly trivial detail, but one that defined my memory of the moment. Not until years later would I understand its significance. It meant Paule was from an upper class family, as were almost all of the students who attended the Lycée. Her father was probably a diplomat or an international banker. It occurs to me now that it likely wasn't Paule's idea to invite me to her party but her mother's who saw in my gesture an opportunity to teach her lovely daughter proper etiquette.

I don't know if my mother realized when she got the phone call that the book had been a bribe to buy myself a friend. She never said. Instead, she turned to practical details that had to be addressed.

First, was the question of how I would get to Paule's house. We didn't have a car and Paule lived some distance away. When my mother understood it would require a convoluted journey by bus, tram and foot, she told me I wouldn't be able to go. "You can't go alone, and I can't take you," she said. "There's no one to watch over Tommy, Maggie and the baby." Gentle and full of sweetness, her voice could barely mask the regret.

When she called Paule's mother to decline the invitation, madame Michaux said she would hate to see me miss the party and would happily arrange for someone to pick me up by car and bring me home.

The next problem was what to wear. Never having been invited to a party before, I didn't have any party dresses. My mother didn't want me to wear the same clothes my schoolmates saw me in almost every day, so off we went to PrixBas – a small discount store a few blocks from our house. We bought a bright red sweater with small golden buttons found amid the sale merchandise, piled onto tables just outside the front entrance.

"You can wear your school skirt and I'll iron you a nice white blouse. The sweater will liven it all up."

On the appointed day, my mother touched up my hair with the hot comb and tied red ribbons, crisply ironed, onto the ends of my two braids. I was all ready to go before noon, even though I wasn't scheduled to be picked up until one. At 12:30 I pulled a chair closer to the bay window so I could see every car that turned onto *Rue Wayez* below. I felt faint with excitement every time one slowed or stopped in front of our house, each time expecting it to be my ride.

An hour passed and no one had come for me. By two o'clock, my mother, betraying no anxiety, called madame Michaux who apologized profusely and said they were delayed but would be there shortly. By three, they still hadn't arrived. As the sun began to set my mother stopped calling madame Michaux and took me away from the window.

"They're not coming," she said. "I wish they'd just said they couldn't do it."

"They'll be here, *maman. J'en suis sûr.*"

"It's almost six – the party's over. They're not coming."

I didn't cry in front of my mother. I waited until we had all gone to bed and the house was dark, then I buried my face in my pillow.

We never again heard from madame Michaux. And Paule never spoke of my absence, which she probably hadn't even noticed. My mother and I also never talked about what happened, about how I had given away a thing I loved in the hope of being included, only to be forgotten. We both tried to act as if there had been no harm or hurt. Later in life when I gave everything I had for professional advancement only to be ignored, I would no longer act as if there had been no hurt or harm.

I have a black and white family photo taken just days before we left for America. We are dressed in our Sunday best. My father and Tommy are wearing jackets and patterned narrow ties. My mother is wearing an elegant linen dress with a jeweled neckline showcasing a single strand of tiny faux pearls. If I remember rightly that dress was red, my father's favorite color. Maggie and I are wearing short-sleeved cotton dresses with white collars. Our hair, which must have just been pressed, is long and loose and held back from our faces by white headbands. I remember choosing the dress I'm wearing from a bag of used clothing brought to the house in the weeks before we left by a white American missionary family. I would wear that same dress on the Pan Am flight that carried me away from the only home I knew.

Photo taken in Brussels studio shortly before family's return to Harlem, 1961.

COMING HOME TO AMERICA

꧁

SIX YEARS AFTER we'd set sail, a Pan Am jet screeched down onto the tarmac at Idlewild, soon to be renamed JFK[iii]. It seemed no sooner had we landed in New York than somehow my ingenious mother succeeded in getting us scholarships to attend Walden, an elite private day school named after Thoreau's pond. At 88th and Central Park West, Walden was located in one of the most elegant neighborhoods in Manhattan. That is when I first realized that Harlem and the projects were not in fact a desirable place to be.

Harlem Hospital was the only hospital in New York City to offer my father an internship. When he finished, he opened an office not far away on the edge of Spanish Harlem where he could capitalize on his talent for languages – he speaks flawless French, Flemish, and Arabic as well as Spanish.

Dad settled in Harlem because he believed he had no other choice. He says no other place would have us – either to work or to live. And that is no doubt largely true – the Civil Rights Act of 1964 had not yet been passed.

30 September 1962 – John F. Kennedy during the crisis at Old Miss University, delivering civil rights speech "giving all Americans the right to be served in facilities which are open to the public—hotels, restaurants, theaters, retail stores, and similar establishments," as well as "greater protection for the right to vote." A year later (22 November, 1963) he was assassinated. (Photo by Abbie Rowe)

Looking back, though, I'm not certain job and housing discrimination were the only reasons we ended up in Harlem. I think Harlem was where my father felt he belonged and knew he was needed.

"Who will care for our people, who will lead by example, if not other blacks?" he would implore friends and colleagues who'd fled to suburbia at the first opportunity. "We'll never have anything if we don't reinvest in our own communities," was another of his frequent admonitions.

Money was also a factor in our staying in Harlem. Supporting six people on a struggling young black doctor's salary wasn't easy. Living in Harlem was cheap, and it was the only way we could afford tuition at the private Manhattan day schools my siblings and I were to attend on partial scholarships. "Education," my father preached at every opportunity, "will be your salvation."

My mother spent months desperately looking for a place for us to live while we camped out in the outer boroughs of New York with a string of relatives and friends, overstaying our welcome at each venue. She wanted something decent – clean and safe – in or convenient to Manhattan where my father would be doing his internship.

Uncle Sol, my mother's brother, had a house in Queens. Aunt Terry was as cold and rigid as her husband was warm and giving. They had two children, a girl named Michele and a son, Sol Jr., nicknamed Butch, who were a few years younger than my oldest brother Tommy and me. I think Aunt Terry was jealous of us even though she was the one with the prized "high-yellow" complexion, the three bedroom suburban house, the car, and the husband who worked for the U.S. Post Office, which was still then seen by most black people as one of the quintessential 'good jobs'. Everything we had could have fitted into the smallest room in her house. Everything, that is, except our hope and our ambition which the entire borough of Queens could not have contained. I think she feared that my family might surpass her own in both achievements and possessions.

Aunt Terry resented everything about us. Understandably, she resented having to share her house. It was Uncle Sol who had invited us to stay with them, and I guess she had been forced to go along. Although compared to the two and three room dwellings we had occupied in Belgium, Aunt Terry and Uncle Sol's house seemed enormous, by American standards of the day it was modest-sized. There were three bedrooms and two baths on the upper floor, a living room, formal dining room which had been converted into a playroom, an eat-in kitchen on the first floor, and a partially finished basement. My sister Maggie shared Michele's bedroom, my brother Tommy slept in Butch's room, and my parents, my little brother Jerry and I slept in the basement. We lived there the better part of that first summer [1962] and into the fall. I'm sure it was a major imposition, which no doubt fueled Aunt Terry's other resentments.

She resented that we could speak French. My youngest brother Jerry who had been born in Belgium and was only three spoke only French. Tommy, Maggie and I were conversant in English, but French was our primary language – the language in which we were best able to express ourselves, the language in which we thought and dreamt. But my mother encouraged us to speak English in preparation for attending American schools, and because she wanted to avoid inciting Aunt Terry.

Aunt Terry's eyes would grow wide with indignation and her thick lips tighten to a lock-down whenever we sprinkled our speech with French words or phrases, which we did unconsciously or because we didn't know the English equivalents, or sometimes deliberately just to set Aunt Terry off. After a few weeks, she demanded that we teach Michele and Butch French but they didn't show much interest and resented us for being in a position to tell them what to do. The only thing they ever learned was the phrase *"Excusez-moi, s'il vous plaît,"* which Aunt Terry would insist they utter before rising from the table after meals. *"Excousie moy sill fuss plate,"* they would say in a mocking, sarcastic tone as they rolled their eyes and pushed away their half-eaten bologna sandwiches, traces of mayonnaise and Wonder Bread lingering on their pouting lips.

Aunt Terry resented our European upbringing, which gave us a reserve not often seen in American children. She especially resented that we liked to read while her own two children preferred to watch television, which we had grown up without. Every afternoon we would settle into the living room with our books – *La Contesse de Segur,* or the Tin Tin and Milou series, or the English language library books my mother was encouraging us to struggle through – while Michele and Butch sat in the playroom, singing along with the mouse-eared gang on the Mickey Mouse club and the dancing, smiling jug on the Kool Aid commercials: "Now it's time to say goodbye to all our company, M-I-C, K-E-Y, M-O-U-S-E;" "Kool Aid, Kool Aid tastes great. Wish I had some. Can't wait." Aunt Terry would express her disapproval of our literary pursuits by marching silently through the living room at periodic intervals, chin thrust forward, eyes bulging, lips pressed tightly together.

I don't have many memories of Uncle Sol that summer. Work kept him away most of the time. Although I don't know exactly how it was we came to stay with him, I somehow always understood that he had reached out to help. There is one memory of Uncle Sol that stands out for me. It was a Saturday afternoon, and I was helping him wash his car out in front of the house. It is an odd thing for a ten year-old girl whose family had never owned a car to choose to do. I remember it was a warm sunny day, just Uncle Sol and me. Maybe I was drawn to the sunshine, which never reached the basement room where I slept. Maybe I was drawn to the gentle kindness of this six-foot-five man with skin so dark it was almost midnight blue. Maybe I was hoping that he would reward me with a ride around the block, just the two of us.

We sprayed the car from the garden hose and washed it down with rags dripping in soapy water from a tin bucket.

"Don't forget the hubcaps. Why don't you do the ones on the curbside of the street? I don't want you gettin' hurt."

"Here, take the hose and give it a final rinse. Start on the roof and work your way down. That a girl!"

When we had finished drying off the car with cloths cut from old towels, Uncle Sol took a handful of the damp squares and ran them over the dashboard and the insides of the doors. I stood behind him trying to get a better look at what he was doing, my hand grasping the doorframe. Easing his large body out of the car, he stepped back to admire his work and slammed the door shut, trapping my hand. I don't remember feeling any pain. It was the shock of seeing only half of my fingers that made me cry out. Uncle Sol yanked the door open and pulled me close in an embrace so tender it extinguished my fear. It's the only time from age four onwards I can remember being held. My father never held me. My mother didn't either. They said they wanted us to grow up to be strong. Instead we grew up anxious and depressed.

"Baby girl, I'm so sorry. I'm so sorry, baby girl," Uncle Sol whispered to me before shouting for my father to come out. Drawn by the commotion, Maggie ran from the backyard and tripped as she rounded the corner of the house, cutting her forehead on the bricks.

I got my car ride that afternoon but it wasn't around the block and it wasn't just me sitting proudly in the front seat next to Uncle Sol. My father occupied that place while I sat in the back with Maggie, her forehead wrapped in gauze, my hand swollen to twice its normal size resting in a bowl filled with ice, as we all drove to Harlem Hospital.

The doctor who examined me was a young, chocolate brown man with a toothy smile and black frame glasses.

"Let me see that," he said kindly.

I laid my hand in his wide, warm palm and he drew it so close to his face I could feel his breath.

"Can you wiggle your fingers?" ... Good. I don't think it's serious. But we'll do an X-ray just to be sure. You're a brave girl. I hear you never even cried."

"My father says we're not supposed to cry just because things hurt a little. He says there'll be plenty of big hurts to cry about when we get older."

I'd said this before having a chance to think. My mother had always warned us not to tell strangers anything about what we discussed or did at home. I looked around anxiously to see if anyone had overheard me betray a family secret. When I looked back into the doctor's face, his smile was gone.

Maggie's cut required three or four stitches, which wouldn't have been so bad if they hadn't had to be redone. She was stitched once by the resident on call and a second time by my father, who was appalled by the quality of the resident's work. My father made me watch as he took out the resident's stitches and replaced them with his own meticulous sutures. All I remember is my sister's tears.

When Aunt Terry learned that we would be attending private schools we were unceremoniously tossed out onto the street days before we had planned to move. She assumed, I think, that this meant my parents had more money than she had been told, and that she had been taken advantage of and played for a fool. She didn't want to hear about our scholarships, or maybe she couldn't see the sacrifices we were making. But we weren't moving into a three-bedroom house in a pretty, leafy suburb. We were going to the ghetto.

We were a large family and didn't have much money but we were a *doctor's* family. That was enough to convince landlords who had reservations about our number and our income to invite my mother to inspect the premises on offer. But we were still as black as ever, and that was enough to cause every decent apartment my mother visited to become suddenly unavailable.

Eventually, my mother gave up looking for a place outside the ghetto and settled for a three-bedroom apartment in the Taft Projects, a newly-built public housing project on the border between black and Spanish Harlem, where we were to live for three years.

I remember running behind my mother one hot summer afternoon around that time. She had spent the morning apartment hunting. As she headed down the empty tree-lined street, her ebony face shiny with sweat and tears, she kept sobbing quietly, "We never should have come back."

My mother was the one who always held things together when our precarious world threatened to come apart, and now she was dissolving into despair. I took her hand and led her around and around the block. All I could think to say was "*Ne pleure pas, maman.* Everything is going to be alright." She was ranting about Negroes, white people, racism, segregation, and injustice. I was a little brown Belgian girl and none of what she said made any sense to me, but I felt like the world had come apart.

We packed what we could into the 1953 Buick, a gift from a distant dying relative. The things that wouldn't fit into the car Aunt Terry ceremoniously sat out in the alley behind her house to be picked up with the garbage. Those things included my bicycle with its chipped silver paint, well-worn leather seat, and chain that slipped. It had been given to me by the daughter of one of my father's expatriate classmates in Brussels when her family returned to the States. It was the only thing of any significance that was mine and only mine. My parents, whose struggles did not allow them the luxury of sentimentality, must have recognized what the bicycle meant to me because they arranged to have it shipped back to the U.S. on the cargo vessel that carried what we couldn't take with us on the plane. That night, as the invectives flew from Aunt Terry's mouth, my father retrieved my bicycle from the alleyway and tied it down upon the open trunk of the car. Just before we drove off, I opened my door, took the small pastry box stacked with a mix of tiny green house plants Aunt Terry had inexplicably handed to me as a parting gift that evening, and put it in the gutter. Then we headed into the night, onto the Van Wyck Expressway, and over the Triborough Bridge, towards our new home.

ABOVE AND BELOW 96TH STREET

❧

*I*T WAS DARK when we arrived at the projects from Uncle Sol and Aunt Terry's house, so I didn't get a sense for the setting until the following morning. At first I was so excited to learn that we would be living on the 13th floor of a 19-storey building. Later I realized the 13th floor in buildings downtown had been abolished – folks down there were protected from misfortune.

Taft Projects, Harlem

I had never been in a high-rise before. When I first saw our apartment, unit 13F, I hopped, laughed, and screamed, running from one end to the other. It had three *real* bedrooms and a bathroom just for us, with a sink, toilet and bathtub all in the same space. At the other end of the apartment, down a narrow corridor there was a galley kitchen with a wall of cabinets, a gas stove, a refrigerator, and, unbelievably, a corner reserved for a washing machine. Off the kitchen was a dining alcove that connected to a living room. Each room had its own radiator and window. The corner bedroom I shared with my sister had two windows.

When I awoke the next morning and looked out through the glass panes framed in naked steel, I felt overwhelmed. I could see from Harlem – an endless expanse of tenement rooftops – to the downtown skyscrapers of Manhattan. The view was so sweeping it made me feel insignificant.

Later that day I went downstairs to investigate the playground in the center of the complex and saw that our building was just one of more than a dozen identical towering structures, all battleship gray. As I grasped the starkness of my new surroundings, I felt even more inconsequential. Even in appearance my new Harlem neighborhood was more threatening, less nurturing.

Running up the center of each building was a stack of eighteen 40-foot long terraces encased in floor-to-ceiling chain-link fence that made them look more like cages. In the years we lived there I never saw a single tenant standing on those terraces. The entrances to the Taft buildings were all so identical and stark. A wide stainless steel entryway led you into a lobby with walls of cream colored tiles interrupted on each side by endless rows of postal boxes and, at back, by two stainless steel doors with small caged windows for the elevators.

That's when I realized we were living in prison-like structures – no softness, no color, no warmth, and no beauty.

There were only two elevators to service a building with over 200 apartments, each of which housed a family of at least three or four. Just getting to the street was a challenge. It would take an eternity to get down to there if you waited for the elevators. They came slowly or sometimes not at all. And you never knew who or what you would find when you finally got on one. There might be a group of the tough kids I quickly learned to avoid. Or there might be a pile of human excrement. And so I ventured out less and less.

Although our apartment in the projects had far more windows than I had ever known, I yearned for that solitary bay window overlooking Place de la Résistance. In the projects, you could open only the top half of a window – but even when it was fully extended the opening was barely wide enough to allow you to dangle an arm out. Except in the sweltering days of summer the windows stayed shut to keep out the black soot that coated everything in sight, and to avoid catching the kitchen scraps and garbage that tenants on the floor above would toss down onto the streets, even though every floor had an incinerator chute. I felt like I was living among animals.

When we first moved into 1735 Madison Avenue we pretty much stayed in the apartment. Then we moved to the playground at the back of our building; to the laundry room in the basement of the building across Madison Avenue; and to the market under the railroad bridge two blocks behind our housing complex. But we didn't really get much beyond a three or four-block radius until we started going to school.

The world I came to inhabit was divided into two spheres separated by 96th Street on the East Side and 110th Street on the West. The ghetto was contained in one sphere, the rest of humanity in the other. In order to get to school we took the Madison Avenue bus to 86th Street and then the cross-town bus to Central Park West. 96th Street was a demarcation line that separated ghetto from the rest of the world. It was a border I crossed five days a week, always coming home to the 'bad' side of town.

The contrast between the two worlds couldn't have been starker. Above 96th Street it was filthy and chaotic. Life was lived in trash-filled, overcrowded streets. Houses were places you escaped from, not places where you sought shelter. Children, many of whom were cursed or discarded, were allowed to run wild. They played in the streets, and in summer even swam in the streets – streets filled with water from hydrants ripped open for relief from the boredom and unrelenting heat.

Men and women sat on stoops, even in winter, hollering at their children and each other. Merchants hawked their wares – both legitimate and contraband – in the streets. Sometimes people died in the streets from gunshots, knifings, drug overdoses, speeding cars, or just plain exhaustion.

Above 96th Street everything seemed old and decrepit. The tenement buildings sagged and reeked of stale air. The grocers sold hardened bread, overripe vegetables, and meat that had begun to dry and turn brown, trucked up from shops below 96th Street where these items had been deemed unsuitable for consumption by white people. Pharmacists sold drugs whose expiration dates had passed – like the asthma medication that nearly killed me.

Below 96th Street was clean and orderly. Life was lived in elegant interiors. The buildings were grand, majestic, and distinctive. Uniformed doormen stood guard under awnings, offering greetings and assistance to those who lived there in tones as soft, warm and deferential as their sideward glances at me were harsh, rude, and contemptuous. The richly appointed lobbies with their wood-paneled walls, European antiques and Persian carpets seemed to draw residents to them like magnets. Even the elevators were wood-paneled and carpeted, often manned by white-gloved attendants.

Below 96th Street merchants displayed their wares behind the plate glass windows of small shops. They sold things I had never seen before or known that you needed.

Below 96th Street little girls were coddled and spoiled. Caroline Kennedy set the standard. After her husband had been shot, Jackie Kennedy came to live with her two children at 85th Street and 5th Avenue, just steps from where I caught the cross-town bus five days a week. I would often see young Caroline, impeccably clothed and coifed in tailored dresses with matching coats and hats that were a far cry from my mismatched hand-me downs. She was either being walked to school by nannies or sitting in the back of a long black limousine, basking in her mother's attention.

As time passed, I came to believe that what made you a 'somebody' or a 'nobody', what made you someone who mattered or someone who mattered not at all, was whether you got on and off the Madison Avenue bus at 96th Street. I became obsessed with the idea of getting myself to the 'good' side permanently. I would dream about climbing on and off the bus at 96th Street on my way to and from school – rich, important, proud, and secure.

All of those who climbed on the bus below 96th Street were white. And so I came to believe that to be somebody I would have to become a white person. But I could not begin to imagine how I might accomplish such a transformation.

Then one day a pair of brown skinned children, a brother and sister, boarded the bus quietly but confidently at 96th Street. "This can't be," I thought. But they were back there the next day and every morning thereafter. These children were chocolate colored like me but had fine features and long, straight, silky hair. I had never seen anyone quite like them. They were like a cross between a black person and a white one. I now know they must have been East Indian but back then I just knew they were the most fascinating people I had ever seen. They opened up a new world of possibilities for how I might transform myself into a 96th Street bus boarder. I decided then that I could join their world if I could just change the texture of my hair. That seemed much more doable than changing my skin from brown to white.

One day my mother mentioned that her beautician had told her about a chemical that would straighten your hair. I pressed her for details on just how straight. I don't remember exactly what she said but I became convinced that someone had finally figured out how I could have "white" hair. I pretended to be only vaguely interested in the news my mother had delivered. But inside I wept with joy and fell to my knees with gratitude for the genius, the saint, who had figured out a way to change me into someone who was good enough to board the bus at 96th Street. I had hope.

I actually did get to live out my fantasy of disembarking at 96th Street, once. On that day, I climbed down from the bus in slow motion, gleefully searching for admiration and envy in the faces of those who would continue on up into the ghetto. For a brief moment, my little chest swelled with pride. But it didn't last long, because of the circumstances that had unexpectedly propelled me off that bus before my destination. That afternoon one of my classmates, a blonde girl I considered my best friend, had joined me on the uptown Madison Avenue bus on her way to a doctor's appointment. I got off the bus with her at 96th Street because I was too embarrassed to admit to her that I lived above it. I pretended that I just wanted to be able to continue our conversation, insisting that it would be "no trouble at all" to walk the few remaining blocks home. She prodded and teased me about just how far above 96th Street we lived, oblivious to my pain, even in the face of my awkward attempts to evade her questions. She went on to her doctor's appointment and I walked the twenty blocks from 96th to 116th Street, weighted down by too many schoolbooks and too much shame.

DOWN SOUTH

❦

OUR FAMILY'S MOST ambitious holiday was in the summer of 1965. We drove from New York City and headed south – six people and a German Shepherd in a sky-blue Chevy II, a tent slung across the roof. Along the way, we were to spend some time "down south" so that we would, in my mother's words, "know where you come from," even though we'd never been there.

The things I knew about "down south" made it a terrifying prospect. I knew that Andy Goodman[iv], who graduated from Walden before me, had gone "down south" on a "freedom" bus ride[v] and been shot and left to rot in a Mississippi swamp along with [Mickey] Schwerner and [James Earl] Chaney. I knew Chaney's younger brother, Ben, made famous by the photograph taken at the funeral of his small, brown, tear-streaked face resting on his mother's bosom.

In the aftermath of the murders, Ben had been invited to the safety of "up north" and given a scholarship to attend our school. I knew from watching television that "down south" people who looked like me were blown down streets by fire hoses and attacked by police dogs when they marched for something called "Civil Rights." I knew from stories my parents told about their childhood, that "down south" was a place of "white only" signs that meant people who looked like me could not drink at water fountains, swim in pools, or sit at lunch counters or on park benches, and could be jailed or killed for challenging these prohibitions. And I thought that we were smarter and better for living "up north" where I could and had done all of those things. So why did we need to go "down south?"

As we neared "down south," I could feel my parents' apprehension growing. My father became more cautious, less sure of himself. My mother grew quieter.

The first incident occurred in Maryland – which until then I had not realized was "down south." We drove up to a campsite and when my father inquired about availability, the attendant with the craggy face who stood inside the small hut at the entrance said, "Well, we ain't never had no 'boys' stay here." My father thanked him and drove on. When we were at what he deemed a safe distance he explained to his puzzled children the significance of that brief exchange and why, out of concern for our safety, he had not protested.

By the time we got to Louisiana, there was no longer any question that we were really "down south," nor any ambiguity about whether we would be welcomed. Somehow, we managed to drive straight into a civil rights protest march on the outskirts of New Orleans. The marchers were proceeding with determination down the highway, accompanied by helmeted police and vicious hecklers. Dad said firmly, "look straight ahead, keep the windows closed, and don't say a word." For what seemed like an eternity I sat frozen, staring straight ahead as I had been told. At one point, I mustered the courage to steal a sideward glance and saw a young boy, his face red with rage, spitting out the words "Niggers go home."

We visited my parents' childhood homes, which, in spite of everything they had told us and we had seen, they remembered as safe and nurturing places. First, on my mother's side, we went to Grandpa Rivers'[vi] house in Mobile, Alabama. The image that's stayed with me is of a white, clapboard house, a swept dirt yard in front, graced by a rusting automobile, and lots of noisy, curious, friendly children who wore no shoes and ran around the outside of the house with a large flying insect tethered to a string. The image that's stayed with me of our visit to my father's hometown of Valdosta, Georgia, is of a gathering in the living room of a worn-down shack, overrun with roaches. My mother says to this day my father remains deeply wounded by the look of discomfort on our faces.

What I learned that summer was that "down south" could be a dangerous place for people who looked like me. It took me years to learn that in many ways "up north" was no better. That it was, perhaps, even more dangerous because there were no "white only" signs to warn that you were not welcome, and there was no family homestead to shelter you.

The stories my parents had told of these places before our journey south had created a picture of an ideal home and family. Neither existed.

STRIVERS' ROW

✿

Strivers' Row *houses are architecturally significant residential buildings in New York, each one a designated landmark. Constructed between 1891 and 1893, developer David King designed them for upper middle class whites. King's speculative development failed, and most of the houses were soon owned by the Equitable Life Assurance Society, which had financed the project. By this time, Harlem was being abandoned by white New Yorkers, and the company would not sell the King houses to blacks. As a result, they sat empty. When finally made available to black residents for US$8,000 each, they attracted hard-working professionals, or "strivers," who gave the houses their current name. By the 1940s, decay had overtaken many of the houses, which were then converted to single room occupancies (SROs). With the post-1995 real estate boom in Harlem, many of these houses have been restored to their original condition.*

After the projects, it was my mother who led us to our new home in Harlem. Pursuing a tiny ad in the real estate section of the Amsterdam News she persuaded the old black woman who owned the house to sell it to us instead of Malcolm X's young widow.[vii] This house was to stay with our family through to the new millennium and draw me back to Harlem one last time as an adult.

"Two-Sixty-Two," as it came to be known in the family, is one of a row of nearly identical brownstones that line both sides of 138th and 139th Streets between Seventh and Eighth Avenues in New York City. Designed by the celebrated architect Stanford White, these grand, turn-of-the-century homes always attracted the more prosperous elements of the community, even during the years when Harlem was so ravaged by poverty, drugs, and violence that it came to resemble a war zone. In the 1940s the two blocks were nicknamed Strivers' Row and the name stuck. Some of them still housed remnants of Harlem's upper crust when we bought Two-Sixty-Two in 1965, and many, like ours, retained much of their original splendor.

Two-Sixty-Two had some fifteen rooms on four floors, including two kitchens, a formal parlor, a more casual living room, a large foyer with a grand carved wooden staircase, a library, and five bedrooms. Every room was graced by a fireplace with a decorative mantel, some of them with built-in mirrors. The high ceilings and walls were covered with intricate crown moldings, and the parquet floors in the public rooms bore exquisite designs composed of woods in varying hues. Brass fixtures from the days of gas lighting were still attached to the walls, as were bells used to summon servants from a street level kitchen with its massive brick fireplace. All of the brass was painted over by the time we arrived, but many of the wooden fixtures retained their original finishes, at least in the formal rooms.

The library of Two-Sixty-Two was on the third floor. An antique wooden desk Mom discovered at Goodwill sat in the middle of the room, a thick, black, rotary-dial phone resting on the edge. Floor-to-ceiling bookcases lined the longest wall in the room. The walls were covered with a golden yellow paint my mother chose for this sun-bathed room.

On lazy summer afternoons I would wander into the library, casually explore the shelves, finding a book of fiction I haven't noticed before. I would settle my adolescent body onto the floor below the window, eagerly anticipating being transported into the rich world of someone else's imagination. It might be John O'Hara's A Rage to Live or another of those musty books recovered from a trunk we'd found tucked away in a dark corner of the basement shortly after moving in.

One afternoon, chin resting in my hands, I sat at the desk, intently studying pictures in J.A. Rogers' dense treatise, Sex and Race[viii]: renaissance style paintings of pitch black men cavorting with full-figured, milk-white maidens with exposed breasts; depictions of Louis XIV's lonely queen with a Negro dwarf who fathered her mulatto daughter; a portrait of Beethoven looking plausibly Negroid. I derived a delicious guilty pleasure from reading the Rogers books, which I soon understood to be forbidden texts. It was not just that some of the pictures were erotic. Rogers' pictures try to prove his point that Negroes were present everywhere in history and in the world and indeed in everyone. I never saw these books anywhere except in our library, and my father, who treated them with a reverence reserved for the Bible, made it clear that this was stuff 'they' don't want 'us' to know.

On cold winter evenings, my mother would sit at the desk, its top covered with papers and files, trying to balance the books for my father's struggling medical practice and trying to decide which of the payments on the household bills could be delayed another month. Surely not the tuition for our private school – the principal was threatening to forbid us from attending classes. Surely not Con Edison – they would not have hesitated to leave another Harlem family in the dark. Maybe Medicaid would finally send the payment for the hundreds of poor patients my father treated so she could pay all the bills on time.

My father would sit rigidly in a chair by the window, legs crossed, left hand supporting his elbow, holding a book about the black experience in America, silently mouthing words that fueled an anger so potent it crowded joy out of every corner of the room.

A speed-reading machine also sat in the library. A contraption about the size of a shoebox, it had rolls of reading material inserted into it and when you turned it on the readings scrolled by a small window on the front of the box. The idea was to take in entire paragraphs as they came into view instead of reading word by word from left to right. As you mastered the technique you gradually increased the speed at which the tape rolled until it practically whizzed past. I spent weeks sitting at the desk with that machine, trying to learn to read faster so that I could earn my ticket out of the poverty and despair that surrounded and threatened to engulf us.

Sometimes I would reach for my father's yearbook from City College of New York. I took this book down, drawn to the hope and optimism radiating from my father's eyes in his graduation photo, and the levity and laughter in his smile in the photo of the football team.

Alongside my father's yearbook were the yearbooks from Walden[ix]. One year's book held the photo of a Beggars' Opera performance Tommy and I appeared in. As MacHeath and Lucy we were standing center stage, kissing. Our lips never did touch. I hadn't wanted to kiss my brother. I was fifteen years old and it was my first time on the stage. Over the course of two evening performances I sung myself voiceless. I so relished the role of the mischievous wench I forgot to be nervous. The thunderous roar of so many hands coming together to honor me when I stepped forward for my final bow made time stop. I stood frozen in the blinding glare of the stage lights unable to see those whose admiration felt like it ran so deep I could have drowned in it. Until that time I had believed that I was not only inconsequential but also invisible. That night I could not fall asleep. I kept reliving that glorious moment and touching my face to reassure myself that I really had come into being.

Tommy's character, MacHeath, was the manly, two-timing cheat and thief the other characters found so irresistible. My character, Lucy, was the woman MacHeath had scorned. Tommy wouldn't learn his lines. As opening night drew near, the cast and teachers directing the play grew exasperated. I grew angry and ashamed. Tommy was making trouble again. When Tommy made trouble, Dad raged and beat him and the harmony I clung to for balance vanished.

I wasn't the one that helped Tommy finally learn his lines. My classmate and other co-star – a girl named Julie who had frizzy blonde hair, crooked teeth, an angelic soprano voice, and played the role of Polly Peachum, MacHeath's true love – came to the rescue. Julie took the subway up to Harlem every day after school for nearly a week and sat on the landing in the foyer of Two-Sixty-Two, reading the script out loud with Tommy over and over again until the words became a part of him. Julie was one of the few Walden classmates to come to Two-Sixty-Two and the only one who came more than once.

In the end, Tommy's performance was also a triumph. Looking at the photograph, I could still hear him singing, relishing and lingering over the deepest bass notes of the mournful dirge MacHeath delivers from his death row cell as he downs a mug of ale:

O cruel, cruel, cruel case!

Must I suffer this disgrace? Of all the friends in time of grief,

When threatening Death looks grimmer,

Not one so sure can bring relief

As this best friend, a brimmer.

Tommy brought the house down when he sang that dirge. Maybe we should have paid more attention. Maybe we should have been alarmed by the fact that someone so young could touch that kind of sadness in himself. Could it be that the fear, loneliness and depression that in the years to come would grip his life had already descended on Tommy? But I loved him and wept when he sang his death row dirge. I later discovered that Tommy had probably started drinking in high school, if not earlier. Mom used to complain that the woman who sometimes helped her clean Two-Sixty-Two was drinking our "whiskey." To my teetotal parents, all alcoholic beverages were whiskey. I think that designation has its roots in my father's love of Western movies with their obligatory saloon scenes of dusty, gruff cowboys quenching their thirst by throwing back shot glasses of whiskey. My parents sometimes got gifts of liquor, which they stored in the cabinet at the bottom of the breakfront in the main dining room. These liquor bottles mostly never again saw the light of day, except on very special occasions when Dad would throw open the cabinet door with great fanfare and invite guests to serve themselves. When Mom noticed that the liquor seemed to be getting suspiciously low, she started putting marks on the bottles. The liquid kept falling below the marks even though no one in our family drank, at least so she thought.

Sundays at Two-Sixty-Two centered on the dining room.

"Come an' eaaaaaaaaaaaaaaaaaat," my mother would call from deep within the bowels of the house, summoning us to gather round the large walnut dining room table. On Sundays we would sit at the table for hours, held in place by the force of my father's bitter, angry sermons.

He would tell us dark tales of his childhood in Valdosta, Georgia – tales of deprivation, Jim Crow, and lynchings. "They killed those two boys for whistling at a white woman. Their families laid them out on a table in the parlor, dressed in their Sunday suits. We didn't have funeral parlors in those days. My grandmother helped support us by taking in white folks' laundry.

A few days after the funeral, some white boys dropped off their families' dirty clothes. My grandfather and I were sitting on the front porch. 'This is for Angie', they said, calling a grown woman by her first name. My grandfather just looked at the ground."

He would launch into a tirade against the misplaced priorities of the Civil Rights leadership. "Those handkerchief heads are running around the country begging white people to allow Negroes to integrate. Our kids don't need to sit next to white kids to learn. We should be asking for money to build up our own schools. White people think Negroes aren't much more than animals. I work myself to death to send you kids to the best private schools in the City and those Jews have your brother playing basketball instead of concentrating on his studies, bringing home a 'C' average. A horse can run! I sent you to that school to study not to play sports."

He recounted the horrors he had seen on the streets of Harlem during the week, as if we need be reminded of how dangerous they are. "Those niggers are speeding down Lenox Avenue in broad daylight, running from the cops. I thought it was a coat flying up in the air. That poor woman was dead before she hit the ground. She looked just like your mother."

The words would spill out of his mouth onto the table, slither around the empty platters, bowls and plates as they made their way toward my brothers and sister and me, and wrap themselves around us, tying us down in our seats. Even Oumar, our fearless dog, sat frozen in place.

My father always sat at the head of the table with the tall windows overlooking the small concrete yard one story below at his back. Wrought iron bars had been installed on these and all of the first and ground floor windows of Two-Sixty-Two to try to keep out thieving junkies. The sun pushed its way through those bars, flooding the room with light so bright it was difficult to see my father's face. But it didn't really matter, because the voice that delivered those sermons conveyed all of the intensity and rage the light kept us from seeing in his eyes.

The first year in Two-Sixty-Two my mother had to prepare our meals in a small space at the back of the dining room that originally housed the butler's pantry and dumbwaiter. The makeshift kitchen had a sink, a gas range, and a small refrigerator. A tall white metal storage cabinet stood against the wall opposite the sink and two shorter cabinets hung on the back wall. A narrow Formica table provided the only counter space. The kitchen was a warm, magical place where my mother turned out elaborate meals that nourished and held us all together – eggs, grits, sausage, and biscuits; fried chicken, yams, and collard greens; beans stew and corn bread; fried fish with corn on the cob; and Jell-O molds; pound cake; sweet potato pie, and bread pudding for dessert.

Sometimes my parents' friends would join us for Sunday dinner at Two-Sixty-Two. On those occasions my father tended not to monopolize the conversation as much as he did when it was just family. Sometimes when we had guests, I would even get to speak. I remember the day we sat around long after the food had been consumed, arguing with my mother's friends, Frances and Lil, and their meek, silent husbands about whether middle class blacks should have stayed in Harlem instead of fleeing to the suburbs. Even though Harlem terrified me, I took my father's side arguing that Frances and Lil had been wrong to flee. Years later my mother called to tell me that Frances had dropped dead on the sidewalk just outside the suburban house where her family had come apart, the house where her husband had turned to drink and her boys had failed and turned to drugs.

As Strong as Colored Girls Need to Be

※

WHEN I NEEDED to ask permission of my mother to do something, I would spend hours or even days formulating exactly how I would pose the question. Usually we spoke in the master bedroom of Two-Sixty-Two, my parents' sanctuary; the place where I relished watching my mother make herself beautiful. It was on the same floor as the library, and Mom had built a cedar-lined closet in the corridor that joined the master bedroom to the master bath.

I went one day to ask my mother if I could have my hair cut. I wanted to be transformed into Miriam Makeba[x], the famed South African songstress with a close-cropped natural hairdo. She was said to be the client of Frenchy the hairdresser Mom used. Mom reluctantly agreed to let me cut my hair and wear it the "Afro-style" popular among so-called black militants. There was a shelf at the top of mom's cedar closet where she would store the things she prized most. And there she put the brown manila envelope that held the remnants of my long, straight hair.

All the children's bedrooms were on the top floor of Two-Sixty-Two. In the closet-sized washroom that was near my bedroom I admired my new style. The washroom had a window that looked out into the shaft of Two-Sixty-Two's two-storied light well. It also had a large deep washbasin that in the early days of the house was probably used for laundry, and a small sink encased in a marble countertop where we brushed our teeth and washed our faces. Usually I didn't linger in this room because the framed mirror that hung above the sink provided too close a view of the gap, buckteeth that caused me so much shame. The wide space between my two front teeth marked me as a Mabry. It had been passed down by someone in that line to generations of offspring including my grandmother, assorted aunts, uncles, cousins. Later it would reach even to my nieces.

I inherited the buckteeth from my mother. Hers lent a look of poignant elegance and she wore them proudly. I thought my protruding gap teeth made me look poor, flawed and ignorant, especially in the company of my private school girlfriends whose smiles had all been rendered perfect by expensive orthodontists.

I trained myself to look away and cover my mouth with my hand when I smiled or laughed, and when I posed for photos I strained to pull my thick lips together. Sometimes I stuffed toilet paper into the gap, took off the thick glasses that robbed me of any chance of ever being thought pretty, smiled fully and gazed into the mirror standing as far back from it as I could. The gap, and the pimply forehead disappeared in the fog of my nearsightedness and the dark pits that were my eyes seemed wider and softer than I normally saw through those Coke bottle lenses.

My parents tried to reassure me I was beautiful just as I was. I didn't know if they believed that or just couldn't bring themselves to tell me they couldn't afford braces on top of private school, dance and piano lessons.

When I got to law school in my mid-twenties I put aside enough money from my lucrative part-time jobs to fix my teeth and get contact lenses. I was glad then that my parents chose to spend what little money they had as they did. The funny thing is that friends say my smile and my eyes are my most engaging features and that I smile broadly and often, and I laugh uproariously.

Still, Maggie always was the pretty one with the almost perfect teeth, and the vision that didn't need correcting, and the smooth, light brown skin. Maggie was the smart one who would win the *Prix D'Excellence* for being first in her class year after year at the Lycée Français and would go to the University of Pennsylvania at age fifteen. Maggie was the virtuoso pianist with her heart-stopping rendition of Beethoven's *Pathétique* and Chopin's *Funeral March*. Maggie was the rebel.

Maggie, although four years younger than me, was always braver. She was never afraid to break the rules. Maggie had boyfriends on the sly, despite knowing that if Dad found out he would smack her and terrorize if not brutalize those boys.

One day Mom discovered Maggie had been exchanging steamy letters with some convict at Sing Sing prison. She beat her with one of our father's belts and Maggie backed off, trying to hide in the closet. She wrapped her arms around her head and curled up so far into the corner of the closet that Mom had a hard time wielding the belt. Maggie lay there coiled up in a tight ball, refusing to cry, refusing to heed my pleas – "Please tell her that you're sorry! Please tell her that you won't do it anymore! " I needed it to stop.

Another day Maggie marched a homeless man she'd picked up on the subway into the house and asked Mom to feed him. Mom marched him right back out, although she did have him wait on the stoop while she fixed him something to eat.

Maggie was more resilient than me. She didn't wither when the roomers who hung out on the stoops yelled catcalls as we passed them. Maggie laughed and dismissed the harmless taunts. "Mmmmmmmmm, there goes beauty and the beast," was their favorite line whenever they spotted us walking Oumar, our vicious German shepherd." I held onto the nasty and the mean ones: "I'd like to get me some of that! What's the matter, bitch, can't you speak? You think you better than me? Fuck you!"

Unlike me, Maggie wasn't afraid to bring her downtown schoolmates to our uptown house. There was a Canadian girl, a diplomat's daughter, whose whole family drove up to Two-Sixty-Two one oppressively hot July day to deposit containers of red geraniums from their Park Avenue terrace in our front courtyard. They wanted us to babysit the plants while they summered in Quebec. Mom was either too polite or too embarrassed to tell them their flowers couldn't possibly survive a Harlem summer.

I was afraid to bring any of my schoolmates home. Amy was my closest friend at Walden and the only friend I ever invited home. On the day of her visit, when the bus crossed 110th Street and all the other white people got off, I turned to see her eyes wide with fear and her mouth open. I knew then it had been a mistake to bring her home. When we got to 138th Street, she practically ran the two blocks from the bus stop to our house, her eyes fixed with a determination that suggested a single sideward glance might keep her from reaching safety.

I took her on a quick tour of the house. She didn't make a single comment. When I offered to make French fries, a food we both loved, she seemed to relax for the first time. We headed for the kitchen where I pulled out the can Mom saved her cooking grease in and started to spoon congealed globs into a pot I had set on the stove. Amy's face took on a sickened look. "What's that? Pig fat?" she said. We never finished making the French fries.

Not only did I have buck teeth, bad eyes and a timid spirit, I also had size eleven feet. One summer I was drawn into my bedroom closet by fumes emanating from a mouse that had lain down and died in one of my patent leather shoes – the pair with chunky heels and a thin strap across the instep I was so proud of, the shoes that seemed so much more elegant than the sturdy, lace-up 'dufus' shoes that were usually the only offering in the stores for teenage girls with size eleven feet, the ones I thought dressed me so nicely until that Sunday afternoon when Tommy declared that they looked like "combat boots." I was glad to be able to use the dead mouse as an excuse not to wear them anymore.

My bedroom, on the top floor of Two-Sixty-Two, was one of two narrow rooms that stood side by side – Maggie's on the left, mine on the right. The floor in both rooms was covered with a royal blue and chartreuse shag carpet that didn't quite go with the elegant pale gray-blue and white traditional girl's furniture Mom had stretched to buy.

In the corner of my bedroom I had my desk, where once I stayed up all night typing a term paper on the Br'er Rabbit[xi] tales because I was tired of writing about Odysseus, Juliet and her Romeo, or Anna Karenina.

My twin bed rested up against the window. On sweltering summer evenings when I couldn't sleep I'd sit up in bed, elbows propped on the sill, and peer lazily up and down the street. One day I saw a long skinny man humping a very large woman with huge breasts in the rooming house across the street. The lone window was open and uncovered, their small room lit by a single naked bulb dangling from the ceiling. He was performing what looked like a round of rapid push-ups, pumping up and down with his skinny arms, and skinny legs straight out behind him. Then the fleshy woman sat or stood up, her breasts jiggling as she straightened the sheets, before lying back down for another round.

The prospect of catching this act again brought me to the window night after night until I saw one man on the landing of the same house plunge a knife into the body of another and I watched a thick red stream snake down the steps onto the sidewalk. I opened my mouth to scream but no sound came out. As the assailant ran, his victim crawled away, and the old woman who owned the place opened the front door and wearily poured buckets of water onto the landing until the water ran clean.

I didn't lean out of that window again until the April night in 1968 when Dr. King was assassinated and Eighth Avenue went up in flames. We all rushed out of Two-Sixty-Two when we heard glass breaking and saw crowds of young men running down the middle of the street. Soon fires were raging in the stores owned by Jewish families[xii]. Tommy foolishly rushed into a clothing store before it was set aflame and came out giggling, carrying a box of children's pajamas. My father knocked him upside the head, made him take it back, and ordered all of us back to 139th Street.

My legs were so busy shaking they almost forgot to support me. When I heard my father say that the flames licking at the edges of the four-storey apartment building that anchored Strivers' Row to the corner of 8th Avenue posed no danger to our house, I believed him. I had to, even though I could see fire trucks retreating in a hail of bottles and bricks. I walked slowly back to Two-Sixty-Two trying not to look unsteady or afraid, and climbed the steps to our front door, grateful for the solid wrought iron railing that held the weight my legs could no longer bear. And then I climbed the wooden stairs to the top floor, entered my room, shut the door, kneeled on my bed, and peered reluctantly out that window, watching the flames, hoping the fire trucks and the world would not abandon us.

My bed was my refuge. I lay awake at night in that bed until I heard Two-Sixty-Two's front door pulled shut by the last one to make it in. I always worried about everyone making it home without being shot, stabbed, or run over by speeding cars driven by bad guys fleeing from the police.

The last one in was usually my father. And after hearing that familiar thud and click and the heavy footsteps in the entryway I fell asleep knowing that tomorrow at least we would eat, and have a roof over our heads, and, most important, be able to go to school because our tuition would be paid.

When I felt anxious and distressed I retreated into my room, lay on my bed and hugged my pillow, pretending it was the warm, muscular chest of a rich and famous adoptive father who adored and pampered me and stroked the long, straight silky black hair I still secretly dreamed I had. For a time the pillow was Kirk Douglas. Then it was Paul Newman. Later it became a black version of Paul Newman.

When my monthly menstrual cramps got so intense I couldn't stand up, I writhed in silence on that sweat-drenched bed, waiting for the hot tea with whiskey and honey Mom taught me to make to take effect, trying not to let Mom see that I was not as strong as she tells me colored girls needed to be.

My brothers also had rooms on the top floor of Two-Sixty-Two. There was a skylight that ran across the full length of the stairwell, withstanding years of winter snow, spring rain, and blistering summer heat. One day Tommy leaned over that banister and looking down toward the landing in the foyer, sprayed a can of Raid at a giant cockroach two stories below, full of false bravado.

The boys' rooms were at the back of Two-Sixty-Two, overlooking the alley. The view from those rooms was harsh with the backs of the houses on Strivers' Row being far less elegant than their distinctive facades. That's why my parents decided the girls should have rooms at the front.

The alley was where residents put out the trash and where city sanitation trucks rumbled through once a week. The alley was the place where thieves ran and junkies nodded out. The alley had at one time been lined with delicate carriage houses. There was still a sign on one of the four columned gates that provided access to the alleyway warning entrants to "Please Walk Your Horses." When we moved into Two-Sixty-Two most of the carriage houses had been replaced by poorly constructed garages. Our carriage house was still standing, but barely. We didn't use it to store anything because it looked like it was on the verge of collapsing and its doors couldn't be secured.

An alley cat once delivered her litter in a darkened corner of that forlorn structure. We took bowls of milk out for several days after we discovered her, so it couldn't have been hunger that caused her to cannibalize her young. I was the one who found the lifeless bodies with tiny, half-eaten heads. It seems she had killed her own kittens to spare them from what she knew would be a wretched life. Maybe that's when it became harder for me to hope.

The door to Tommy's room bore a large gash that someone, I can't remember whom, put there when they kicked it in a fit of anger. Tommy was always making somebody mad. Tommy used to hide nudie magazines between his mattress and box spring. I don't know how I discovered them but after I did I would sneak into his room and hurriedly leaf through their glossy pages before carefully replacing each one exactly as I'd found it. It would be years before I actually had sex, and it rarely matched the sweetness of those virginal arousals.

TOO WHITE AND TOO BLACK

✿

*M*Y PARENTS DIDN'T 'spare the rod', but they used it more on my two brothers and sister than me. It wasn't fear of pain that kept me from engaging in behavior that could provoke a whipping, but a fanatical aversion to discord.

I can recall only two beatings I received – one from my mother and another from my father. Each time I was struck only once. Mom hit me for trying not to be like black people. Dad hit me for aspiring to be like one of 'them.' Straddling privilege and poverty, I found myself to be both 'too white' and 'too black' for my parents.

My mother slapped me on a Monday morning in September 1964. We were standing in the living room of our apartment in the Taft projects arguing about stockings. We had been back in the States less than a year and I was having difficulty navigating between the two worlds I inhabited – the world in and around Walden, and the world around the Taft Projects.

One of the first things I noticed was that the girls in my class at Walden, all of whom were white and lived in large, elegant pre-war apartments with maids quarters, and doormen standing guard in their front lobbies, wore stockings to school. By contrast, the Harlem girls, who lived in projects that were more like prisons than homes, or in dark, sagging tenements, wore thick white socks rolled down around their ankles. Although I hated the garter belts you had to entangle yourself in to wear them, I decided I needed to be in stockings, too. But Mom decreed that at twelve years old I was far too young to wear stockings to school every day. I could wear them only on Sundays or on special occasions.

That Monday morning my mother and I stood by the living room windows arguing about stockings. As she lectured about not wanting me to "grow-up too fast," I looked away in anger and frustration, staring out the soot-streaked windows while the undesirable end of Madison Avenue bustled thirteen stories below. I could make out clusters of black girls heading off to school in their white socks.

Suddenly and unexpectedly, a defiant impulse seized me and spun my head around toward my mother so that I looked straight into her eyes. My arms were pressed stiffly against my sides. "All you really want is for me to dress like those black girls down there," I blurted out loudly, the shrillness of my twelve-year-old voice dampened by insecurity and uncertainty.

Mom's hand leapt out of nowhere and slammed into my cheek. "Those black girls down there?" she screamed. "And just what do you think you are!"

I stood frozen, unable to speak, my arms pressed even more firmly against my sides. I was trying to read her face to decide what my next move should be. It was strangely contorted. She looked mad, shocked, and sad all at the same time.

We stood there staring at each other, until our anger dissolved into regret. I regretted having caused the mother I so adored such anguish. I think she regretted having hit me, regretted that we had been required to even have such a conversation, and, as I learned years later, regretted that we had come back to America.

Neither of us spoke. Sensing that regret was about to dissolve into tears, I hurriedly collected my schoolbooks from the table and headed out the door, my white socks falling around my ankles.

My father slapped me on a Sunday morning five years later in the spring of 1969. We had by this time moved from the projects to Two-Sixty-Two. We were standing in the ground floor living room, my father lecturing me about how blacks were never going to advance and why I shouldn't be hanging out with black folks who were going nowhere.

The night before the confrontation with my father was an exceptional time. With no really close friends among the blacks of Harlem or the whites at Walden, I didn't fit in either world and had begun to master the art of solitude. But that night I had gone to a party, one of the only parties I can recall attending in the seven years I lived in Harlem. It had been in an apartment of an upscale condominium high-rise at the north end of central Harlem.

I can't recall whose house it was, and perhaps I never knew. The party had been organized to celebrate a successful performance of the National Black Theater Workshop, a newly formed troupe of which, at seventeen, I was the youngest member. Twenty or so actors in our group had come together to dance to Motown 45s and enjoy some light refreshments.

I had long since stopped going to parties given by my schoolmates because I was never asked to dance. As I whirled and jerked around the living room to the sounds of Marvin Gaye and the Four Tops, I felt embraced and included for almost three hours that evening and only reluctantly left the party so that I could make it home before my midnight curfew.

Mom had given me permission to attend the celebration. Dad hadn't been around for me to ask or for her to consult him. When he learned what we had done, he erupted in a fiery rage that climaxed when I came down to breakfast the following morning.

As he lectured me, I tried not to listen and at the same time look like I was. I stole occasional glances out the street level window, looking through the wrought iron bars at the feet and legs of men, women, and children making their way along the sidewalk as Strivers' Row came to life that Sunday morning. I tried to distract myself from the ugliness of the moment, imagining the bodies and faces that belonged to those feet and legs, trying to guess where those strangers might be headed. But my father's voice was so insistent, so full of self-righteousness, bitterness and indignation that I could not shut it out.

As the lecture progressed from general to specifics – from all black people to the particular black people I had chosen to associate with – with a tone of revulsion and look of pained disgust he started to deride the companions who had allowed me to feel, if only for a moment on that one Saturday night, that there was a place where I belonged. Against my better judgment, I decided to speak out in their defense.

"I didn't do anything wrong! We just danced! The people whose house the party was at were perfectly decent people! They had a really nice house!"

Dad's right arm swung like a baseball bat and his elegant surgeon's hand landed on my face with such force it knocked off the thick-lensed glasses that had caused me so much shame, and sent my whole body flying to the floor.

The room was suddenly out of focus. I couldn't make out my father's face but I could still hear his voice. "How dare you suggest that anyone has a nicer house than mine!"

That wasn't what I'd said or even meant but I knew better than to protest. I also knew I needed to be able see clearly so I crawled around on the floor, fumbling for my glasses. I found them smudged with oil from my adolescent face and one of the stems broken off, unable to get them to sit straight on my face.

My mother's shadowy figure appeared beside my father and she admonished me for talking back to him. I kept my silence and my distance from both parents that Sunday morning, and would do so for another twenty years. It wasn't until I was nearly fifty that I realized my father had been afraid – afraid for himself, afraid for me, and afraid for all of us.

Placing us in private day schools on the Upper West side, my parents urged us to excel so that we could 'rise above' our circumstances, which meant not ending up like the folks we saw all around us in Harlem. We were also urged, however, to develop a strong identification with and loyalty to our race, never betraying or abandoning our people. It was a balance I would spend the rest of my life trying to perfect.

LEAVING HARLEM

❦

IN THE SUMMER of 1969, just before leaving for Mt Holyoke[xiii], I got a job as a sales clerk at Bloomingdale's – only because they accepted the lie that I had no plans for college.

The first thing I bought with my earnings was a three-piece Samsonite luggage set in champagne-colored vinyl. Over the course of that summer I'd fill those suitcases like a bride would fill a hope chest.

I bought a red turtleneck from Gimbels, and a yellow pullover with thick tan corduroy pants from Alexander's. From my own counter at Bloomingdale's, I sold myself a fringed navy scarf I'd been eyeing for weeks. I bought a calf-high, fleece-lined pair of boots I thought I'd need for those fierce New England winters but quickly abandoned once a fellow Mount Holyoke girl said they made me look like "Nanook of the North." I bought a three-speed hair dryer I'd use to keep my Afro puffed-up in a twelve-inch halo. And finally, Mom and I tracked down a small specialty shop on Madison Avenue where we bought a sheepskin coat – the incredulous blonde shopkeeper seemed almost reluctant to sell it to us.

My friend Vina built a hope chest that summer, too. Hers was a real trunk, which Mom and I helped her pick out from dozens we surveyed at as many thrift stores. Vina and I were both getting out. She chose Howard University in Washington, D.C. I was going to Mount Holyoke in the heart of the Connecticut River Valley.

Vina was the only friend from my Harlem years I remained in contact with after I left for college. She was murdered by her husband in 1975 – stabbed repeatedly and left to bleed to death in the hallway of her father's high-rise condominium in the Bronx. The last time I saw her, she was patched up and laid out at the back of a dingy funeral parlor on 110th Street, around the corner from her father's barbershop. She was clothed in the orange bridesmaid's gown she had worn to her sister's wedding.

1969/70 Linda around time of Mt Holyoke

Maybe Vina got killed because Howard wasn't far enough away.

My father gave everything he had and more to his practice in Harlem, struggling to generate enough income to support all six of us. He might have fared better if he'd been willing to run a "Medicaid Mill[???]," like many of the other doctors in Harlem, but he wanted to care for and heal his patients. He would spend hours listening to tales of unspeakable deprivation because he understood there were no prescriptions or other medical interventions for what truly ailed his clients. Too often he would carry the burdens they unloaded on him home, and too often those burdens got laid down at our dinner table. Over liver, onions and mashed potatoes, over fried chicken, greens and cornbread, over peas and rice, over pound cake and bread pudding with rum sauce, we heard the tale of the seven-year-old boy who brought his three-year-old sister to the office because she was burning up with fever and he knew he couldn't count on his absent parents to save her; of the young woman who was disfigured but not blinded by the lye her boyfriend threw in her face; of the old man for whom loneliness was a worse affliction than his crippling arthritis. "So be grateful for what you have," my father would always say, as if we need be told.

In the end my father couldn't compete with the "Medicaid Mills." He wasn't making any money. And although those he healed and comforted were deeply appreciative, others in the community – the young men caught up in the epidemic of drugs and crime who were beyond healing and comforting – kept trying to kill him for money and drugs. His office was robbed at least half a dozen times, twice with him in it. His car was broken into so often he finally removed the "MD" license plates he had once so proudly displayed. He was so frequently accosted when he made house calls on patients too sick or too old to make it to the office that he stopped carrying his leather physician's bag, replacing it with a cheap briefcase, and started carrying a gun. After supper he would gather up his briefcase, pack his pistol, and on his way out the door declare, "I may have to take a life to save a life." He would smile or even chuckle when he said this, but his voice sounded weary and afraid.

One afternoon, when he was sitting in his office waiting for the next patient, three young men burst in and held a shotgun to his head. "Give it up you bourgeois nigger or we'll blow your head off." They took the cash, boxes of syringes, and ripped the watch from his arm, the only luxury item my father ever owned.

I don't know if my father begged them not to kill him or not to take his watch. He never said. I do know that not long after that he gave up his practice on the edge of Spanish Harlem. He took a job at a methadone clinic for a while, but he had never wanted to work for anyone but himself and he despised the addicts he was charged with treating. Finally, he gave up on Harlem.

In Harlem, as my father had struggled to build a healing, compassionate, and financially viable practice in a community plagued by deprivation, we children struggled to learn the language and customs of two new, alien worlds – black America and white America – and tried to understand why everyone who looked like us was warehoused, unseen and forgotten, in a place of want and danger and despair. Why did only whites live in the sumptuous world south of the Harlem border that we migrated to daily to attend school? As my mother struggled to keep us whole and we all struggled to keep from being swallowed up by the epidemic of drug addiction and crime that was sweeping through the streets around us, we filled Two-Sixty-Two with our dreams and our fears, our laughter and our tears, our anger and our silence.

One by one in the 1970s, we children left to go away to college. I went off to a New England women's college and then on to graduate school and law school in Washington, D.C.; I wanted to be seen and heard, I wanted to be someone who mattered, I wanted to make a difference in the lives of all the world's dispossessed, and I wanted to live in a place that was pretty and safe. Eventually I settled in the San Francisco Bay Area where I became a partner in a prominent corporate law firm, and then a professor of international law at Stanford University.

It was at Stanford that I finally came to realize that despite all of my apparent successes, I was trapped in an abyss; one deeper, darker, lonelier, and far more dangerous than the ghetto I had left behind. On an unseasonably warm October day some thirty years after I had left the house on Strivers' Row, I ended my career through an angry and very public resignation from Stanford.

STANFORD NEWS

STANFORD
NEWS SERVICE

NEWS RELEASE

07/20/93

CONTACT: Stanford University News Service (415) 723-2558

Mabry, expert in international trade and business, joins Law School faculty

STANFORD -- Linda A. Mabry, an expert in international trade and business transactions, has joined the faculty of Stanford Law School. Her appointment as an associate professor became effective July 1, 1993.

Mabry was previously a partner in the San Francisco law firm of Howard, Rice, Nemerovski, Canady, Robertson & Falk. She was offered a regular teaching position at Stanford after spending the autumn 1992 term at the school as a visiting lecturer in residence.

"Linda Mabry brings unusual international and legal strength to our faculty," said Paul Brest, dean of Stanford Law School, in announcing the appointment. "She will play a key role in preparing our students for a future in which business, trade and information are increasingly global."

Mabry, who is African American, was born April 30, 1952, in New York City and raised in Brussels, Belgium, where she attended the Lycee Francais. She returned to the United States during her teens, graduating from Manhattan's Walden High School.

During her undergraduate studies with Mount Holyoke College in Massachusetts, she spent a junior year abroad at Makerere University in Uganda. She graduated from the Massachusetts school magna cum laude in political science in 1983.

Mabry then earned a graduate degree from the School of Advanced International Studies of Johns Hopkins University (M.A., 1975), followed by a law degree from Georgetown University Law Center (J.D., 1978).

While in law school, she received a teaching fellowship and served as an editor of a Georgetown scholarly journal, Law & Policy in International Business, and executive editor of the Association of Student International Law Societies' International Law Journal.

Fluent in both French and Spanish, she also worked during this period as an interpreter for the U.S. Department of State.

Her first positions after completing law school were as an attorney-adviser in the State Department (1978-80) and then as a special assistant to the general counsel of the U.S. Department of Commerce (1980-81).

Mabry then entered private practice, first as an attorney with Hogan & Hartson and then with Miller & Chevalier, Chartered, both of Washington, D.C.

From 1981 to 1986 she also was a performing member of the Arlington Dance Theatre, a dance company based in northern Virginia.

She moved to California in 1986 to become managing attorney of Helm & Purcell of Oakland and joined the Howard, Rice firm in 1987.

Mabry's scholarly publications include Export Controls as Instruments of Foreign Policy, which she co-authored with Homer E. Moyer Jr., a former general counsel of the U.S. Department of Commerce. The book was published in 1987 by the International Law Institute.

She is a member of both the District of Columbia and California bars. A leader in her field, she has served on the executive council of the American Society of International Law and is currently a member of the American Bar Association's sections on international law and business law, California State Bar's sections on international law, business law and intellectual property law, and other professional groups.

Beginning this fall, she will be teaching a course in international business transactions.

Now a resident of Mountain View, Calif., Mabry has traveled extensively in Europe, Africa and Latin America.

Mabry's appointment brings to three the number of African Americans on the permanent faculty of Stanford Law School. The 45- member professoriat now also includes 10 women. Mabry is the second African American woman to win a tenure-track position.

Article by Constance Hellyer, Stanford News Service press release, July 20th 1993[1]

---

[1] Used with the generous permission of the Stanford University News Service.

The Exceptional Outsider

Self-Respect, Not Happiness, is the Reward

I was like Catherine Sloper in *Washington Square*, one of those characters who according to Azar Nafisi, "depend to such a high degree on their own sense of integrity that for them, victory has nothing to do with happiness. It has more to do with settling within oneself, a movement inward that makes them whole." For us the reward for standing up for oneself, for one's principles, is not happiness but a new found self-respect.

— *Reading Lolita in Tehran*

THE ONLY ONE

DURING MY TWENTY year legal career I moved from one job to another – from the public to the private sector, from practice to teaching, from Washington D.C. to the San Francisco Bay Area. The jobs, one more prestigious (if not always more lucrative) than the next, came easily. Contentment proved far more elusive.

On the eve of the new millennium I gave it all up for good – the law, my professorship at Stanford University, the fast track and the mainstream. Now by day I work as an administrator in a small, affordable housing non-profit, while at night I write, trying to make sense of it all. Looking back on those years I have struggled to understand why I ended up in places that were so utterly wrong for me; why, even after I realized I was a misfit, I fought so hard to stay.

In all of those places I was almost always the "only one" – the only African American, the only African American woman, sometimes even the only lawyer of color. Sometimes I was the "first one" as well as the "only one." When there were others we were always less than a handful and, even then, the "other ones" – especially the African American women – usually left long before I realized that I, too, could not stay.

For a time my singular status gave me a perverse sense of satisfaction. I was doing something no one who looked like me had ever done, something that everyone thought was impossible. I was a pioneering hero, driven forward by the same intoxicating mixture of fear and exhilaration I imagined fueled the conquests of the white men who were the first to climb Everest, fly solo across the Atlantic, or journey into outer space to set foot on the moon. What I failed to understand until it was too late is that living in world where you don't see yourself reflected back causes your soul to atrophy to the point that life becomes unsustainable.

The sense that I was special was reinforced by those in charge. They seemed to view me with awe. My arrival and continuing presence was a constant cause of celebration. A result of which was that as much as I longed for company, I had mixed feelings about a "second one" ever joining the organization. My status would be diminished. I would no longer be unique or special. I would cease to be the focus of so much attention.

I had an intuitive feeling that there was only room for one black woman partner or tenured law professor. They couldn't handle more than that. Having one in their midst assuaged their liberal guilt, allowed them to present themselves to the world as an institution that valued diversity. Two might be a prelude to an invasion, a take-over. How many times did I hear comments like, "Is this a conspiracy?" "You guys plotting a rebellion?" when two or more of my colleagues of color and I gathered together and headed out for lunch. The white men who made these comments chuckled when they spoke, as if it were a joke. But their forced levity was always tinged by hints of fear and condemnation.

This established a dynamic in which we were afraid not only to champion other women and people of color, especially African American women, but we didn't even want to be seen together.

How else can I explain the response of Condi Rice[xv] to my suggestion that we have lunch? Condoleezza Rice was the Provost, the chief academic officer, at Stanford University in the 1990s. I was a tenure-track professor in the Law Department. Out of 1,600 tenured and tenure-track faculty, there were never more than a half dozen black women at any given time. I called Condi's office one winter afternoon and, as expected, didn't make it past her secretary. I told the secretary I was calling to see if Condi might be free for lunch sometime. The secretary said she would relay my request to the Provost and get back to me. A few days later the secretary called to inform me that Condi had said she could have lunch with me in four months, on a Wednesday in spring. On the appointed day, when the winter rains had ceased and the hills around Stanford were adorned with orange poppies, yellow suncups, royal blue larkspur, and white star lilies, the secretary called to inform me that Condi was ill, "female problems" she whispered. Lunch would have to be cancelled. In the weeks that followed the hills turned brown, the wildflowers vanished, and our lunch was forgotten.

Kim Taylor-Thompson[xvi] also kept her distance. The first black woman to be a member of the permanent Stanford Law School faculty, she had joined the faculty shortly before me and would be gone within two years of my arrival.

A New Yorker profile[xvii] of Caroline Hoxby[xviii], a rising young economics professor at Harvard, illustrated the point. Most blacks, including myself, would consider her black. But she was careful to distance herself from that part of her heritage, emphasizing that her father was only part African American, the other part being Native American. Many African Americans, myself included, can also lay claim to Native American ancestry. Still we consider ourselves and are considered by white America to be black. That's the oldest ruse in the book. There is even a running joke about it. "Yea. You Indian. A Black Foot!" In America black and anything else makes you black. Period. When the police stop you they don't hyphenate. Her mother is described as a woman of "Eastern European extraction." That they didn't say 'white' leads me to believe that she must be 'mixed.' When asked about her racial identity Professor Hoxby equivocated, saying that she thought of herself as both black and white.

As a Rhodes Scholar at Oxford, Hoxby authored a prize-winning thesis in which she argued that for minorities, investing less in education is a rational decision since job discrimination makes the return on their educational investments uncertain. She now dismisses this idea as "probably wrong."

I was dismayed to read that she laughed when asked if she had ever been discriminated against and said only in Oxford where she felt like a colonial. At the same time she conceded that "most men in economics think that women aren't very good at math, aren't very rigorous, and aren't very good at theory. You have to prove to them that you can do these things." She had a dizzying array of hobbies, all of which one would associate more with a white woman of privilege – French cooking, gardening at her eighteenth century Victorian farmhouse (I assume she wasn't growing collard greens), listening to classical music – Palestrina being her favorite composer – burying herself in 19th century novels – she was currently reading Henry James, and rescuing stray animals, subsisting on coffee and four hours of sleep. Yet when asked what drove her to work so hard she said she didn't know.

Her conservative views on government intervention and market competition have made her a "political darling" of the right. I expect she will go far.

It is not only women of color who fail to support other women. Judy Swain[xix], chair of the Stanford University School of Medicine, was profiled in the Palo Alto Weekly in early 2000, no doubt a public relations ploy by the university to improve its image in the aftermath of several public blows to its claim of gender and race equity. "Stanford has been as friendly as any place I've been." Could it be that we had been at the same institution? I suppose if I was chair of a Stanford Department I would have felt compelled to say the same thing. She lives three thousand miles from her husband who is dean of the school of medicine and vice chancellor for academic affairs at Duke. "It's not ideal, but during the week we don't have time to be married. She flies to Durham North Carolina on the red-eye on Thursday evenings "after a day of working from 7AM to 7PM, rushing home to feed the cats and pick up her suitcase which is usually packed the night before, and making a quick jaunt to Fitness 101 to get in her daily workout." On her office wall is a photograph commemorating the day she accomplished what she called her "greatest dream": landing a plane on an aircraft carrier. In her spare time, she works on her golf swing.

Although my arrival and continued presence had been a cause for celebration, it wasn't until years after I had abandoned the fast track and the law (and I finally had time to think) that I realized their expressions of glee had more to do with congratulating themselves than with honoring me. Those who considered themselves to have been instrumental in my hire praised themselves for having had the foresight and courage to "take a chance" on me. White liberals were the most gleeful. It seemed to reinforce their sense of innate moral goodness. They were doing their part to advance the cause of 'social justice.'

By embracing their constant praise of me being "exceptional," I was embracing an implicit judgment that the overwhelming majority of those who looked like me were utterly lacking the qualities and skills the institution valued. I was exceptional because I wasn't like all those other black women. I now realize that I was a collaborator. By allowing them to hold me up as the singular exception I was helping to shore up a system founded on the belief that black women have no worth.

I had once believed that the awe they seemed to express at my presence was a sign of the esteem in which they held me. But it wasn't awe, it was astonishment – a kind of disbelief that I could really do the things they did. And it was inspired not by their esteem for my abilities but arrogance rooted in a deeply held conviction that the talents I possessed were supposed to be unique to people who looked like them.

The look I would inspire when I performed some feat I wasn't supposed to be able to perform – like speaking in full, articulate sentences about international trade policy – or sometimes simply by my presence in a place I wasn't supposed to be – like sitting in the faculty lounge at Stanford Law School – was the sort of look you would expect to see come over the face of a man whose dog walks into the kitchen one morning, pours herself a cup of coffee, takes a seat at the breakfast table, unfolds the *New York Times* and after glancing at the headlines asks her master what he thinks about the Bush administration's proposed elimination of the tax on corporate dividends.

When he recovers from the initial shock, the owner prides himself on having had the insight to select such an exceptional dog. He congratulates himself for rising to the occasion and welcoming the dog as a member of the family.

They reacted as if my presence upset the natural order of things. I came to understand that displays of competence or independence made them feel anxious and insecure.

I remember the day I delivered a paper on a major law review article I was writing at the faculty lunch meeting. I'll never forget looking out across the room as I came to the end of what was an impeccable presentation. Before me lay a sea of pale white faces – some bore faint smiles, others had looks of puzzled uncertainty, others a look of pained relief that I had not let them down, still others genuine encouragement. The face of one professor who sat at back of the room glowed red, like a volcanic ember. He had waited until the end to pose his question. It came in the form of an accusatory statement that ridiculed my thesis and ended in a period. Later when I reluctantly submitted my manuscript to him for a courtesy review, he responded with eight single-spaced pages of comments containing not one word of praise, except to note that the topic I had chosen was an interesting idea. He couldn't even find it within himself to give me credit for having thought of it. It was obvious he hadn't really read the piece, but merely scanned it for scattered points about which he thought he knew more than me.

I had seen a similar look of anger on the face of another colleague at a student organized conference on international environmental law. After my smooth, articulate presentation, Tom Heller[xx], a colleague who would loom large in my future at Stanford, sat in the room and seethed. I don't know if he was more angered by the fact that my performance was so well received or that the students had not asked him to chair the plenary session. He didn't try to sabotage my presentation then but I think that moment might have been the start of what drove me from academia and the law. The next time we found ourselves on a panel together addressing alumni, he would humiliate and marginalize me by usurping the conversation and prattling on about grandiose plans for the international law program I'd heard nothing about. I thought he was exaggerating for the alumni. It would be another two years before I realized that they weren't exaggerations, and that, in fact, discussions were being held from which I was excluded.

When I thought they were in awe of me I felt flattered. When I realized they were astonished, I felt patronized. I realized how empty their praise was. I was a token. They praised me but they didn't include me. They trotted me out for the dog and pony shows that were put on to woo clients to the firm or donors to the law school. But they couldn't find me when they landed a client or secured a grant.

GIIIIIRL, WHAT THE FUCK YOU TALKIN' ABOUT?

INTELLECT IS THE key currency in the academy. As a professor, your worth is defined largely by how colleagues rate your intellectual prowess. At Stanford Law School the principal arena for public display of one's cerebral abilities was the weekly colloquium, the infamous "Wednesday lunch." At noon, professors would gather in the faculty lounge to listen to a colleague present a work in progress.

Together with faculty meetings and graduation it was one of the few events professors were required, or at least strongly encouraged, to attend. A number of my colleagues needed no encouragement. They would never miss an opportunity to show off and maybe even add to their stash of currency by spotting the fatal flaw in a presenter's argument. Some were so addicted to the occasion that they dragged themselves to those lunches even as their bodies failed under burdens of age and illness. The Wednesday lunch was almost like a hazing ritual. Professors were rude and cruel. Questions were frequently delivered with an edge so sharp I thought the presenter might actually bleed. More often than not, they were designed *not* to prod the presenter into thinking differently or more deeply about a particular point, but to demonstrate how much the questioner knew about the topic.

Sometimes the speaker would be the one inflicting pain. She would torture her audience with language so abstruse, concepts so abstract, that they were threatened with the ultimate harm – proof positive that the speaker was smarter than them.

By the time I joined the legal academy, its scholarship had already become so arcane it was impenetrable. It was like attending a lecture in a language so foreign I couldn't even begin to guess at the meaning of its words. I remember one talk titled, "A Deweyan Perspective on the Economic Theory of Democracy."

... The basic methodological premise, as for economics, is a rigorous atomistic individualism. The basic moral stance, as for much of economics, is that this is positive

theory, unconcerned with the goodness or badness of political actors and institutions, but only seeking to observe how incentives and institutional structures interact to produce empirical consequences.[xxi]

I didn't have a clue what Peggy Radin[xxii] was talking about. But I later came to understand that, in all likelihood, no one else did either, not even those who engaged in the verbose exchanges that followed.

On the warm October afternoons I sat listening to preposterous exchanges, I missed the streets of Harlem where people understood that life is precarious and they had no time for bullshit, where people had no place to hide their poverty or pain, where people related to each other with a raw but vital directness. If I had had the courage to reveal that part of me, I would have sashayed up to the podium, cocked my hip, looked Peggy dead in the eye and with a perfectly timed dramatic pause said out loud, "Giiiiirl, what the *fuck* you talkin' about?" To this day I regret not having done so.

But I didn't, and neither did anyone else, because we all knew that to do so would be viewed as an admission that you had not understood the presentation and risk diminishing your stash of currency.

I did see someone challenged in this way once, but only once. A tenured female professor from Stanford Law School had invited me and the other faculty women to her home for an afternoon tea – given in honor of a visiting female professor from another law school. Janet Halley[xxiii] was in general a kind and thoughtful colleague, although I wouldn't have considered her a friend. She was also someone so concerned about offending any norm that she never articulated a firm position on any matter. She always looked and sounded like she was drowning in ambivalence. She had become so adept at academic-speak that even her conversational speech was unintelligible. I didn't know the visitor, so I can't say if it was her usual manner to be confrontational. I think the visitor had at some point applied to join the Stanford Law School faculty and been rejected, so it may also have been that she simply felt she'd earned the right to be a 'bitch.' (There was some additional back-story to which I wasn't privy.) In any event, the group became engaged in animated conversation about something having to do with the law or the academy. When the hostess went off on some tangent with great verbal flourish and it appeared she would go on endlessly saying nothing, or at least nothing anyone could grasp, the visitor looked at her with thinly veiled contempt and said the dreaded, forbidden words. "What are you talking about?" Our hostess froze for just an instant, her mouth parted in the shape of the word she'd been about to pronounce, then launched immediately into a clarification that was even more obtuse than her original statement, and far less fluid or certain.

It was like sitting in the bleachers at a tennis tournament. All around you people's eyes are riveted to the match, their heads moving from side to side in unison, in rhythm with the players' strokes. Your fellow spectators offer commentaries on the state of play, exclaim at a point well-scored, gasp at the long, masterful volleys. But as far as you can tell there is no ball. You think you're going blind or insane. So you have your eyes checked. There's nothing wrong with your eyes. You eventually find the courage to discreetly ask one of the other spectators if they actually see a ball, and she confesses to you that, in fact, there isn't one. You feel both reassured and terrified by that confirmation. You realize that you're surrounded by people who have lost touch with reality but have so much invested in having secured a seat to attend what they believe to be the match of the century that they might well kill you if you broadcast to the world that it's a ruse, a scam, a phantom match with no ball.

I remember one Emeritus Professor in the days before he finally succumbed to Parkinson's disease, wheeling himself and his portable oxygen tank into the lounge on his electric scooter. Watching him distressed me. Was his world and life so limited that he could think of no better way to spend his dying days than attending Wednesday lunches? Is that what it meant to become one of them?

I found myself acknowledging that he might have found it stimulating, that it might have given him a reason to hang on. But why didn't I feel that way about these occasions, about my work as a lawyer and law professor? Was there something wrong with them, or something wrong with me?

In an environment dominated by people who refer to themselves as the "smartest people in the world," I had to be hyper vigilant about making sure I never came across as anything less than brilliant. The pressure this engendered was paralyzing. Maybe that's why I never heard Kim Taylor-Thompson utter a single word at the Wednesday lunch. That is surely why I didn't speak up at one of those gatherings until I'd been on the faculty for months. I don't remember what I said on the occasion of that first intervention, or even when it was, or who was speaking that day. But I knew that if I didn't speak soon, I never would. I had seen the same dynamic at play in my classes. Students who had not heard their voices in the classroom by one third of the way into the semester – usually women and African Americans – would never speak.

Even a casual aside at a social event was well thought out. I would rehearse it silently in my mind while trying to listen to the conversation and gauge the sensibilities of the participants so I could launch my *bon mot* at just the right moment, and in just the right tone. I knew when I'd scored by the look of slight surprise on their faces, bafflement even, with a self-congratulatory subtext: *The Negro spoke, and she was articulate, intelligent, and apposite. How clever of us to have spotted a talented one!* That look, which passed so quickly it would have been missed by anyone except an outsider with acute powers of observation, was followed by genuine laughter, never too uproarious of course, or solemn nods of agreement, depending on whether my interjection had been humorous or serious. Those moments gave me hope that over time I might come to be seen as one of them.

My Impeccable Manners

❧

BY THE TIME I arrived at Stanford I had already developed the impeccable manners of an outsider who wanted at all costs to assure the insiders that she was worthy of being asked to join the club, and that they could count on her to be well-behaved.

After every dinner party I sent elegant notes written in fountain pen on fine stationery – "Thank you for your warm and generous hospitality. It was so kind of you to invite us into your home."

I even sent a "thank you" note to Ken Scott[xxiv], who barely spoke to me before or after he invited me to his large, sumptuously furnished home to enjoy a fine meal prepared by his wife, whose family money I was led to believe allowed Ken to live so well. There were three or four other guests that weekday evening, none of whom I knew, all white male professors from other Stanford departments who, like Ken, were connected to the Hoover Institution, (the conservative think tank housed in a towered building that dominates Stanford's architectural landscape).

It was a month or so before the November 1992 presidential election. As we started on dessert, Ken, resting back in the host chair at the head of the table, elbows on armrests, hands crossed in front of his chest, commanded that we go around the table and each "professional" offer his or her views on the upcoming election. Mrs. Scott, who was seated to her husband's right, eagerly leaned forward in her chair and began to speak. "I think ..."

"I asked for the professionals' opinions," Ken snapped. "Well you could say I'm a professional," she offered meekly. "A professional housewife."

In the chill that followed, Mrs. Scott sunk back in her seat and blushed apologetically. I had just placed a forkful of pastry in my mouth and couldn't bring myself to swallow. I don't remember what I said when it came to my turn.

In December 1993, I sent a photo card to my colleagues wishing them a "Joyous Holiday Season" and announcing my marriage in October to

Dieter Folta, a native of Germany I had met a few years earlier. The ceremony was at home in our garden in the presence of family and a few close friends. Few if any colleagues acknowledged receiving the card announcing my marriage. Only one commented on the photo of Dieter and me standing under the weeping willow tree – me in the golden wedding dress smiling broadly, him in a dark navy suit, chest and chin proudly jutting forward.

Linda and Dieter, 1993

Another time I sent a thank you note to Ian Ayres[xxv] for having Dieter and me to his house for dinner one Friday evening, shortly after I'd joined the faculty. The dinner had been scheduled a week or so in advance. There were two or three other guests, young graduate students or junior faculty as I recall. After Ian poured us each a glass of wine, he stood in the center of his small living room and said cheerfully: "Well, what would you like to eat? I've got some left over noodles in the fridge. Will that do?" We were barely done eating the cold noodles when Ian announced that he would have to leave in twenty minutes because he had a plane to catch.

I sent notes of condolence on the death of family members I had never met and hadn't even known existed – "With deepest sympathy for the loss of your son." Sometimes I even attended the funerals. The wife of one colleague sent me a card thanking me for the "kind note on the occasion of the death of Joe's father." All of my other meticulously crafted notes expressing sympathy for the loss of a colleague's loved one went unnoticed and unacknowledged. Maybe that wife wrote me because she was an Asian married to a white man and had also developed impeccable outsider manners.

Their lack of response made me anxious. Maybe I had violated some strict unspoken code about the limits of familiarity that my powers of observation had failed to detect. Maybe I had crossed the line delimiting what I should have known was inviolable personal space.

Despite all my efforts at socializing with colleagues, I never made any true friends I could count on among those with power and influence in the institution who could protect me and help advance my career. The friends I made left the organization.

In October 1996 I dutifully attended the memorial service for the thirty-something daughter[xxvi] of a colleague[xxvii] who was killed in an automobile accident while on holiday in England. The synagogue was packed. That setting brought home for me how many of my law school colleagues were Jewish. They were obviously comfortable and familiar with the rituals. The men wore yarmulkes with customary ease. My own awkwardness and uncertainty in movements and gestures must have betrayed that it was my first time in a synagogue.

The light oak casket was closed and there was no photograph displayed of the young woman whose name I can no longer recall. As her family and friends walked up to the podium one by one, feet heavy with grief, and delivered tearful eulogies, I struggled to conjure up an image of the young woman at the center of the stories they told – stories about the moment of her death – how, true to her altruistic and optimistic nature, she asked the emergency workers to tend to the passengers in the vehicle she had struck head on, not realizing or perhaps not caring that she was herself gravely injured; about how she decorated the walls of the home she had recently bought with framed photos from her travels and filled its rooms with cooking smells, and friends, and laughter; about how every weekend she went to Hobies, a popular Palo Alto eatery known for its oversized portions. If she resembled her parents and her brother, she was I imagined, an overweight, blonde homely girl. To this day, I have no idea if I imagined her correctly. Still, by the end of the service I felt as if I knew her.

When the service ended I headed straight for my car, half a block away, without speaking to anyone. Unable to bring myself to start the engine I sat and watched the mourners pour out of the temple. Reflecting on their eulogies, I realized that no one had said anything about where the deceased went to school, what she did for a living, how much money she made, what professional awards or recognitions she might have received, or any of the things that had been the nearly exclusive focus of my life's energies. For the first time it occurred to me that maybe I didn't need to be a Stanford law professor to be somebody, to be loved, to be remembered.

AN ALIEN, UNNATURAL WAY OF BEING

꧁

I WAS TRYING to fit into a place inhabited by people whose way of being in the world was alien to me.

People never said what they meant or felt. Honesty and directness, particularly in communication with one's superiors, were discouraged. This resulted in costly inefficiencies. No one wanted to challenge the "big guy," to tell him that what he was proposing was a stupid waste of time. Take Larry Rabkin[xxviii] at Howard, Rice[xxix]. Everyone would always wait for him to speak and then follow his lead. When I once suggested that votes be kept secret I was met with an incredulous stare.

Displays of emotion were seen as damning evidence of a lack of the desired level of self-control. In the world where I had grown up, people were demonstrative; they showed anger and pain and gladness. These people were so reserved I sometimes wondered if they even had emotions. But black people don't have the privilege of dispassion. In the end I was overcome by a rage that has been more than 400 years in the making, the rage that Jimmy Baldwin said every Negro alive has in his blood, the rage he said is like a chronic disease that one is never free of, that can recur at any moment, the rage he said feels like "a kind of blind fever, a pounding in the skull and fire in the bowels." [*Notes of A Native Son*, 1955]

The view that dispassion was the preferred state carried over into work itself. So in the academy being a public intellectual who spoke out passionately against injustice or tried through her teaching and scholarship to effect social change was frowned upon. But I was a product of the Civil Rights era and had gone to law school because I believed law was an instrument of social change. And I felt an urgent need to help pull those of us who were left behind to safety. When I told Barbara Fried[xxx], a fellow law professor at Stanford, that I wanted to write things that made a difference, she looked at me as if I was the most naïve person she had ever come across.

People never talked about the ugly, dirty little truths. But where I had grown up, people didn't have the physical means to keep all the dirty parts at bay and saw no need to do so with words. In Harlem, there was no place to hide your shame. Everything happened in public view. That way of living forced people to have a certain kind of openness and directness and, even though I had been encouraged to "rise above that," I missed it in the academy.

People were often simply not 'nice.' The way they treated others went beyond disrespectful to the point of being brutal and abusive. I went out of my way to be kind, especially to support staff. I think I was trying to compensate for the mistreatment they suffered from my colleagues. But I was also trying to stay true to values I had been raised with – "treat everybody fairly and look out for the little guy." I wanted to be seen as kind, courteous and respectful. It was a way of affirming for myself that I was not losing all of who I was.

They were so devoid of opinions, emotions, and passion it seemed they had no personality left. They almost didn't seem real. Their codes of behavior were unspoken. I didn't know the rules and they were never explained to me. I survived by sheer force of will.

The dirty little secret is that the gatekeepers define the content of 'merit.' They will adapt subjective definitions to give themselves broad discretion, which they then use to exclude anyone who doesn't look exactly like them.

Hard work with excellent results was no guarantee of advancement. Fitting in and getting along mattered more than being the best at what you did. And that meant networking and socializing strategically. I watched plenty of mediocre people in institutions that bragged about their selectivity and the excellence of their employees and work product. I found it hard to develop relationships with people I had nothing in common with, and found uninteresting or even repulsive because they were in a position to further my career. It went against the kind of honesty in human relations I had grown up with. Ingratiating myself to people I had little respect for felt like backsliding. That's why I had worked so hard so move up in the world: so I wouldn't have to kiss ass to stay alive.

Your work is by its nature intangible and only has value if others in the institution say it has value. A single negative remark by one who was perceived to have power could render meaningless an idea or paper you had taken days, months, or years to produce. I remember the young African American applicant whose candidacy evaporated when a professor who had established himself as one of the institutional arbiters on this subject, although I was never quite sure why his opinion was so valued, noted that the young man's work had not been cited by anyone he knew, referring no doubt to the small circle of Jewish men who considered themselves the sole authorities on the subject. In another case, the candidacy of a woman of color lost ground when one of the arbiters (who was not well known beyond a small club of Jewish business law professors) questioned the value and importance of her work because she had not cited him. The young woman was ultimately not offered a position but the work they were so critical of eventually expanded into a book that became an international bestseller.

People boasted about their accomplishments in ways I found unseemly, and rarely acknowledged others' contributions to their success. They took full credit even for things that were plainly the result of collaborative efforts.

People demonstrated a sense of entitlement and assuredness about their lofty place in the world that was foreign to me. White men who didn't make partner or get hired to teach at Stanford were as stunned at having been rejected as I was at having made the grade. At the University of Miami where I was a faculty visitor in 2000 after leaving Stanford, more than one professor came to my office, shut the door and told me about how but for some tragic oversight or run of bad luck or more typically because of affirmative action that favored women and minorities, they would have been teaching at Harvard or Stanford. Some even asserted that they were on their way there, even though they had been at Miami for decades and were unlikely ever to be invited to join another faculty. When I heard this I always thought to myself, 'In all the places I had been women were significantly underrepresented and I was invariably the only African American woman and often the only person of color. So where were all the women and minorities that had taken the jobs that were rightfully theirs?'

I betrayed myself not with lies but with silence. I said I was from New York and that I had gone to Walden but I was silent about living in Harlem. I acted like I had been going to the theater and ballet all my life and remained silent about Mom patching that ugly gray coat we'd picked up at Goodwill for me to wear when I went to see my first play. I acted like I had grown up ice skating and stayed silent about a whole day spent scouring the thrift stores on Third Avenue, searching for skates to wear to a class outing at the Central Park rink, and having my classmates make snide comments about those useless skates with their disintegrating leather and dull blades. I acted like I had always dressed well and remained silent about the church group that came to our house with a bag full of used clothes so we would have something to wear on the flight back to America, or about being nearly fourteen before I got my first new outfit. I showed off my French but didn't talk about running out of food, or cooking on a coal stove, or storing perishables on the window ledge, or sharing a bath with a whole building full of tenants.

The exceptional outsider who is allowed into the inner sanctum of the privileged and powerful and wants to be invited to stay develops acute powers of observation. Mine became so keen I was able to detect the subtlest nuances of the insiders' gestures, speech, and patterns of social interaction. I studied them with the intensity of an actor examining real world characters in preparation for a performance.

I became a pro at deciphering styles of dress so I could replicate them. It's a habit of which I haven't been able to cure myself. My first time in a new place I always feel terribly self-conscious. I always observe the dress so I can try to replicate it so I'll at least look like I fit in. It's led to obsessive shopping trips trying to find the dress or shoes or coat that is just right. I've ended up with lots of stuff in my closets that no longer work because of where I'm living or working.

Learning to read the insiders was a matter of survival. I had to avoid at all cost offending them with my behavior or frightening them with my presence. To do that, I had to develop a finely honed appreciation of their sensibilities. Once I had accomplished that, I would know what kind of person I needed to become.

The goal was to ensure that when they looked at me they didn't see black because that would conjure up all the negative stereotypes they believed defined black people and justified our exclusion. Which meant, in effect, that the price of admission was self-betrayal.

One option was simply to recreate myself in their image so that when they looked at me they saw themselves reflected back. Strategically that would have been the best choice. The problem was, as I looked around me at the other women on the faculty, I didn't see anyone I wanted to emulate. I didn't want to be like Janet Alexander[xxxi], who'd had a heart attack on her way to tenure and had become so stiff I thought she might actually break. I considered modeling myself after Barbara Babcock[xxxii], the first woman to join the Stanford Law School faculty, who was loved and admired by many of the students, until I sensed that our male colleagues held her in disdain. I admired Kathleen Sullivan[xxxiii] for excellence in teaching and in scholarship and for her willingness to go against the grain and take a stand as a public intellectual. But Kathleen had led a tortured life, with one foot in the lesbian closet and the other trying to march towards the seat on the U.S. Supreme Court she so desperately wanted. Deborah Weiss, who was untenured like me, appeared so terrified and uncertain I feared for her health in body and mind. Janet Halley had become so adept at academic-speak that even her conversational speech was unintelligible to me. Ellen Borgersen[xxxiv], the brilliant Supreme Court clerk and former MOFO[xxxv] partner appeared to have lost her ability to write when she entered the academy, and after several painful years took herself off the tenure track and eventually returned to practice. I felt Kim Taylor-Thompson, the lone black woman on the faculty, was making herself invisible to everyone including me. She would be gone within two years of my arrival.

So I decided to construct my own unique and original persona. I would be the model of perfection: brilliant, articulate, poised, elegant, collegial, well mannered, and productive – everything black people weren't supposed to be.

Throughout my years at Stanford Law School I felt like I was standing center stage in the spotlight during the performance of a play for which I had not rehearsed or learned my lines. I didn't even know the title but I was trying valiantly nonetheless to act out my part – not only the soliloquies but also the parts that involved interaction with other characters, all the while praying that the audience wouldn't notice that I was entirely out of place.

It was an exhausting way to live. It was all about me becoming like them. They weren't interested in the real me because they always assumed a colored girl had nothing to teach them.

DEATH OF A LAWYER AND PROFESSOR

꽃

In 1998 I COMMITTED professional suicide. It was really more like a mercy killing, though no one would have guessed that I was deathly ill. The act that brought it all to a quick end was surprisingly uncomplicated. I swallowed an overdose of reality, vomited up the truth, and then it was all over.

The first sign that things were about to go terribly wrong came on September 15, 1998. I was in my office at the Law School preparing to teach my International Law and Economic Development (ILED) seminar, a course that was closer to my true passions than most of the work I had done in all my years as a lawyer and law professor. These were the subjects I had pursued so fervently through nine years of undergraduate, graduate, and law school because I thought it would put me in a position to save the world. But I got sidetracked. I became a corporate lawyer – a partner in a high-powered, prestigious San Francisco law firm, an international dealmaker. And then I went to Stanford Law School to write about it and teach the trade to brilliant, ambitious, and naïve young law students eager to follow in my footsteps. My principal courses were "International Business Transactions" and "International Trade Law", which were more about how to make the world safe for the U.S. corporate hegemony than about how to save it. I relished the semesters during which I taught the ILED seminar.

As I was reviewing my notes the phone rang. It was my mother calling to tell me Grandma Bert, her mother, had passed away just moments before. I cried not for Grandma but for Mom who was devastated even though Bert had been a mean and selfish woman to the very end. The only thing I ever wanted to emulate about Bert was her longevity. As she reached her mid-nineties, my siblings and I would mischievously joke among each other that she was lasting so long "because even God didn't want her." Her passing threw me off kilter nonetheless.

In my drive for perfection I had set for myself an inviolable rule that I would always be in class at least five minutes before it was scheduled to begin. Even my mother's grief did not justify an exception. So I told her I had to go, hung up the phone, gathered my notes, and went off to teach the class.

In spite of my own persistent doubts about my abilities as an academic, I had quickly become an outstanding teacher with a devoted following. But even after five years of superlative student evaluations, my anxieties about giving a less than stellar class persisted. As I made my way across the breezeway to the building that housed the classrooms, I was ashamed to be feeling grateful for the unexpected gift of a fine excuse to offer up if the class did not go well.

The next day, September 16, 1998, I learned that one of my favorite students, a brilliant young Korean woman pursuing a Ph.D. in law, had committed suicide. Jong Min had taken every course I taught. Most students scrupulously avoided sitting in the front row of the sprawling halls where lecture classes were held because they feared it would increase their chances of being called on. But Jong Min always sat there, directly across from the lectern I rested my notes on and sometimes grasped for reassurance. She sat on the edge of her seat, her round face framed by her dark, perfectly straight and evenly shorn hair. She eagerly volunteered answers to my frequent questions posed to the whole class. I would lean toward her in those moments as I strained to decipher her thickly accented English that became even harder to understand when she got braces on her teeth. It was well worth the effort. Her responses were always flawless, original, and thoughtful.

On the first day of my Economic Development seminar, I always asked students to tell their classmates and me why they were taking the course. Jong Min had said with an enthusiastic, slightly bashful smile, "I'm here because I'm Professor Mabry's greatest fan." I was moved almost to tears to know that there were at least some people in that institution who valued my contributions.

I learned from speaking to Jong Min's friends that afternoon that, not unlike many women and especially women of color, she felt alienated at Stanford Law School. Suicides are always complicated matters, but I believed that this fact contributed to the crisis that led Jong Min to end her life. She had asked me to be her thesis adviser and I had declined, citing a self-imposed rule of self-preservation that I would not serve as a Ph.D. thesis adviser for any student until "after tenure." She had signed up with a white male colleague and apparently had received little guidance but plenty of humiliation. She got stuck in the development of her thesis paper and panicked. A few months before she died she had said to a close friend, "Everything would be alright if I could work with Professor Mabry."

Jong Min had been dead for almost a week when she was found. It was the smell that drove them to pry open the door to the room she had barricaded herself into. The smell was still clinging stubbornly to the walls weeks later when friends attempted to retrieve the draft of her thesis from her computer in a futile effort to persuade the university to grant her a posthumous degree. No trace of any of her work was ever found.

When I heard all of this, a wave of grief washed over me and dragged me so far out to sea I didn't think I would make it back to shore.

Not a single professor knew this exceptional young woman well enough to say anything of note about her to her family or at the memorial service. I could not attend because I was helping my mother bury Grandma Bert.

Mom always said that death comes in threes, and there would be a third traumatic event that Fall. It was Friday October 9, 1998. In spite of the events of the previous weeks, I was feeling uncharacteristically good about my life as an academic. My classes were going well, my research was moving along, and I was going to present papers at important conferences at the University of Toronto and the University of Connecticut. I sat in my office that afternoon, warm air drifting in through the open window, the sky bright and cloudless. I had just returned from a quick excursion to the law school library, which stood in the center of the building that housed faculty and administrative offices. I had gone there to retrieve some research materials I would need for the weekend. On my way out I had stopped briefly to talk to a student. My colleague, Professor Tom Heller, appeared out of nowhere, typically distracted and hurried, and stepped between us without excusing himself. He said to me, "I'm putting together some materials on international business law courses at the Law School. Can I use your name?"

I had always found Heller's rushed manner laughable, and considered him to be one of the least productive members of the faculty by the standards for teaching and scholarship that I had been told I would have to meet to receive tenure. No one I spoke to quite knew what he did other than frequently travel abroad, staying in four star hotels and eating in five star restaurants all on law school time. He had never taught or written about international business law. He had in recent years taught a seminar called "Legal Uncertainty" to a class of three students who reportedly found it unintelligible. He had never written anything of note, and had done precious little writing in some 20 years[xxxvi].

Every time he opened his mouth in faculty meetings, I would notice eyes roll. I got the impression he was intimidated by my presence at the law school, perhaps because I knew a great deal more about the subjects he could only pretend to be an expert on.

I was annoyed at the rudeness of Heller's intrusion and puzzled by his question. I thought to myself: "I'm the only one teaching this subject at the law school. Who else's name would this fool use? And what in the hell is he doing putting together materials on my subject area? I guess it's for an internal memo or some administrative materials describing international course offerings." So I said, "Sure, Tom. You can use my name. I'm happy to help in any way I can." Heller hurried off, on his way to nowhere as usual, I thought, while I returned to my conversation with the student. That encounter, which lasted less than a minute, would set off a nuclear bomb in my world.

When I got back to my office and settled into the chair behind my desk, I heard a friendly, rhythmic rap on the door and as soon as I shouted a welcoming "Come in" Elspeth [Farmer[xxxvii]] leaned her head of flaming red hair into the room and in her rapid-fire manner of speaking said, "Got a minute?"

Elspeth was a Visiting Scholar who had been at the Law School for about a year, trying to finish an article about how the German courts handle domestic violence cases. I loved Elspeth. She was the only true friend I had made in all of my time in those hallowed halls.

With a mischievous smile on her face Elspeth whipped an orange flier from behind her back and said, "I saw this on the student bulletin board down by the lockers in the basement. I hadn't heard you talk about this as one of your projects. I couldn't resist pilfering one to show you."

I was curious but not alarmed as I reached across the desk. At the top of the page in bold black letters the words "ANNOUNCING THE NEW TRANSNATIONAL BUSINESS LAW PROGRAM" stood just above a logo, a sketch approximating a flattened map of the word encircled by lines ending in arrows to suggest that they were whirling around the globe. The language on the bottom half of the flier invited "ALL STANFORD LAW STUDENTS" to "AN INFORMATIONAL MEETING WITH PROFESSOR THOMAS C. HELLER AND SUSAN LIAUTAUD." I had never heard of Susan Liautaud[xxxviii].

Elspeth said, "Did you know anything about this?"

"No, " I responded.

"Do you think the fact that you didn't know about it has any implications for your tenure?"

"Of course not! Don't worry Elspeth. I'm on track. I have strong support across a broad spectrum of the faculty. I don't know of anyone at this point who opposes my getting tenure. I really don't think I have any enemies."

As Elspeth left my office, I walked out behind her, flier in hand, and headed to the Dean's office. Dean Paul Brest[xxxix] was standing in front of his executive assistant's desk in the anteroom to his suite of offices.

I held the flier up to him, inches from his face, and said, matter-of-factly, "Paul. What is this? Do you know anything about it?"

Paul responded with a look of mild surprise and puzzlement. He said he knew we'd received money from Coca-Cola, and that he'd have to look into it and get back to me.

Paul is a thin, frail man whose soft-spoken, hesitant demeanor makes him appear shy. That such a man should rise to be the Dean of the second highest-ranking law school in America had always baffled me. Until that afternoon I had trusted Paul. He had aggressively recruited me to join the faculty and persuaded me to stay every time I had thought of leaving. I had believed that he was my greatest supporter. Still, I had always been uncomfortable in conversations with Paul. Whenever we spoke, his eyes darted about the room nervously, looking everywhere but into mine. What I failed to appreciate until it was too late is that his elusive manner wasn't shyness, but the makings of a betrayal that would shake me to my very core.

It was four o'clock. I returned to my office and prepared to leave for the day. As was my custom, before shutting down my computer I checked E-mail. There was a 'broadcast' from Paul to everyone on the faculty that had been sent earlier in the day. In it he announced that the Law School had just reached its $75 million fund raising goal and that one of the gifts that got us there was a $1million grant from the Coca-Cola Foundation for the "Transnational Business Law Program." The message went on to thank Professors Tom Heller and Joe Grundfest[xl] for their work in getting the money.

When I read that message I started to put everything together: Heller's cryptic request about "using my name," the flier, and the Dean's response to it. Perhaps Heller wanted to be able to say that he had discussed the Transnational Business Law (TBL) program with me and that I had endorsed it. I had to question Paul Brest's honesty when he said he knew nothing about the program announced on the flier. I had been duped.

I was the only member of the faculty who had significant practice in international business law, the only one whose teaching and research focused exclusively on international business law, and the only one who was a nationally recognized expert in the field. I had been invited to join the faculty for the explicit purpose of developing an international business law curriculum. I was also the only woman of color on a faculty of nearly 45 professors and only the second one in the institution's 110-year history. (Kim Taylor-Thompson, an African American woman who had been the first, joined the faculty shortly before me and had left by this time). Heller's TBL program was, as far as I knew, the first time a specially funded curricular program was being headed by someone other than the resident faculty expert in the field.

I knew the Law School had been trying to get some money from Coke. Two years earlier, Paul had imposed on me to meet with representatives of the Coca-Cola Scholars Foundation to help persuade them to make a contribution to international law programs at the Law School. But, as I was now learning, he hadn't even had the decency to notify me that we had secured the grant, let alone asked for my input on what kind of programs the funds should be used to support.

In that moment I knew with an unshakeable certainty that this would be the last stop for me on that train traveling to what I thought was the top of the world. I would have to disembark and leave all of my work of 25 years, everything I had and was, behind. For a brief instant I felt an overwhelming sense of lightness. Then, an ominous presence I could feel but not see, wrapped itself around my chest and neck so tightly I couldn't breathe. That feeling of being squeezed and suffocated would stay with me for three years. The feeling of weightlessness would not return until a year later when I became so ill I almost died.

I decided to confront both Paul and Tom directly about my exclusion from the TBL program and arranged to meet with them early the following week. Powerful men are unaccustomed to being challenged, at least by the likes of me. In our meeting, they both lost their composure, and then their gazes became fixed and vacant. Their faces turned red then white and then red again, as if their blood had forgotten which way it was supposed to flow. Then it began.

Tom claimed to have sent me a memo about the program, even though he was unable to produce it. He also claimed he had done it all for me – "in the hope that some day you might take over the program," he said gazing past me – even though I knew far more about international business than he ever would. Paul claimed that he had been trying to "protect" my time even though he had recruited me to be the minority presence on countless committees and at innumerable gatherings that had little direct relevance to my teaching or scholarship.

The unspoken implications of these assertions, which spread through the law school like fire through tumbleweed, were that I didn't read or respond to my mail; that I was immature and inexperienced; and that I didn't know how to manage my time. Barbara Babcock, the senior woman on the faculty, added fuel to the flames by suggesting to the Dean that I was overreacting due to the stress of seeking tenure and caring for a husband with multiple sclerosis, as though I were having a bout of hysteria.

When it became clear that I wasn't backing down, Paul invited me to his office and asked what he could do to make things right. I suggested he start by issuing a public apology. He said that he would see what he could do at the next faculty meeting, scheduled to convene the following Monday.

Paul opened the meeting by speaking so softly and so briefly on the matter that I almost missed it. He said I'd seen a poster announcing a new curriculum initiative in international business law, and was upset, and that he was sorry. Heller, jumped in with his own *mea culpa* so quickly that he almost drowned out Brest's apology. He went on far too long and repeated the claim that he had done it all for me. The interminable reruns of this scene that have played in the theater of my dreams these past years are considerably more dramatic. They always feature Heller beating his weakly clenched fists against the breast pocket of his tweed jacket and tearing at this thinning, disheveled hair.

I stood up and launched into a monologue of my own.

"I know how difficult it is to admit when we have done something wrong, especially in this public a way. So I want to start by accepting the apology offered by Paul and Tom. I want to make clear, however, that this is not about an administrative screw-up. I want this faculty to think about the history of faculty of color at this law school and what it says about how we have been treated – how we have been marginalized, excluded and demeaned. How we have been invisible."

"You know, it takes 250% of who we are to do this job well – and we don't all do it well. You can't ask someone to give that much and then treat them this way."

"Some of you have told me that what happened to me had nothing to do with my race or my gender – that some white men also have been marginalized and excluded. My position is that this should not happen to anyone on faculty. But it does. And it happens consistently to people of color. And when it happens to those of us who are hanging on at the margins by the skin of our teeth, the consequences are devastating."

I sat down.

Miguel Mendez[xli], the sole Latino on the faculty and, at that point, the only minority ever to have been promoted to tenure from within Stanford Law School, rose slowly and said: "I just want to say one thing and that's Linda speaks for me."

The rest of my colleagues, who as was the custom at these meetings had drawn the chairs scattered around the faculty lounge into a broad, slightly irregular circle, sat frozen, their eyes projecting that by now familiar fixed and vacant stare. A few attempted to mask their stunned confusion with nervous half-smiles. They were all so immobile and so silent I thought they couldn't possibly be real. Only one other colleague showed any understanding of my situation, Bill Gould, at that time, the only tenured African American at the law school.

I resigned my position at the Law School in December 1998 and hired a fearless lawyer named John Marshall True. When the students learned of my departure they protested and the press picked up on the story. When reporters started calling to ask me why I left, I told them the truth.

STANFORD NEWS

HOME

Stanford Report, February 17, 1999

Law School grapples with how to increase diversity among faculty

BY ELAINE RAY

On Friday, law school Dean Paul Brest will meet with the school's Faculty Appointments Committee and its four-student liaison committee to discuss new steps the school might take to promote diversity. The meeting will be the second discussion to take place in less than two weeks with regard to the status of women and minority faculty at the school. On Feb. 10, Brest called a town hall meeting to discuss issues of diversity with students.

Increasing diversity at the law school "has been an ongoing process for the 30 years that I have been at Stanford," said Brest, who will step down as dean at the end of August.

Such concerns have been at the center of many discussions on the campus in recent months. Linda Mabry, an associate professor at the law school, resigned at the end of fall semester alleging that women faculty and faculty of color are held to a "higher," "stricter" standard than their white male counterparts at the law school and at the university as a whole.

"What we're asking for is not preferential treatment, but an elimination of preferences that have long been the privilege of white men. What we're asking for is not preferential treatment but equal treatment," said Mabry, insisting that the specific circumstances of her departure were important only to the extent that they fit a "pattern of practices that has resulted in women and minorities feeling marginalized, demeaned and excluded." Mabry is one of several faculty who have filed a formal complaint with the U.S. Department of Labor.

Brest emphatically declined to comment on Mabry's case, but agreed to talk about the law school's record of affirmative action. Brest said that with women representing 25 percent of the law school's faculty, "we are the strongest" among the university's peers in terms of quantity and quality of women scholars. Brest noted that in terms of African Americans and Latinos on the faculty, "there is no top school that is more diverse than we are." Currently the law school's faculty members of color include one Latino tenured professor and two tenured and two non-tenured African American professors -- all men. He acknowledged that there is room for improvement.

Mabry, who was previously a partner in the San Francisco law firm of Howard, Rice, Nemerovski, Canady, Robertson & Falk, was appointed to a tenure-track position in 1993 after spending the autumn 1992 term at the school as a visiting lecturer in residence. She earned her undergraduate degree in 1973 from Mount Holyoke, where she graduated magna cum laude in political science. She earned a graduate degree from the School of Advanced International Studies at Johns Hopkins University in 1975 and a law degree from Georgetown University Law Center in 1978. After law school Mabry worked at the U.S.

90

Department of State and also the Department of Commerce.

At the time of her appointment, Brest praised Mabry for her "unusual international and legal strength to our faculty. She will play a key role in preparing our students for a future in which business, trade and information are increasingly global."

But since then, Mabry, the second African American woman in the law school's history to be appointed to a tenure-track position, says she began to wonder whether her expertise and experience were valued. Despite her background in international business law, she said, she was not consulted about the establishment a new Transnational Business Law program at the school. Instead, she said, she found out about the program from a flier on a student bulletin board.

"I had always had a sense that perhaps Stanford Law School was a dangerous place for me, and that was largely based on my perception about the way the institution treated people who looked like me: that they weren't staying; that they weren't being promoted; that they weren't being given positions of power and importance in the institution. Every hour of every day you walk out into a world where people challenge your intellect, where people challenge your competence and challenge your humanity," Mabry said, likening the last five years at the law school to running a race while pieces of lead were being thrown in her boots. "Then you're asked to run a race against white men who are sailing along on the winged feet of white male privilege."

Brest said that "we aspire to more, especially with respect to the goal of having tenured women of color." He said that at the town hall meeting he explained to students the criterion that all faculty must meet. "Somebody needs to be essentially one of a handful in [his or her] field," he said.

Brest noted that the mentoring of junior faculty also is a concern. The school has a formal mentoring program that requires junior faculty to have two senior faculty members with whom they meet regularly to discuss their progress. One of the suggestions that came out of the Feb. 10 meeting was to have a neutral party look at the school's efforts to mentor and support junior faculty, particularly those who represent minority groups. "One suggestion was that we seek somebody from outside the law school to see whether we are providing an atmosphere conducive to junior faculty success," Brest said, noting that "it's often very useful" to have someone who is not entrenched in the school to assess such efforts. SR

Stanford News | Stanford Homepage

Article by Elaine Ray, Stanford News Service press release, Feb 17th, 1999[2]

Afro-American Faculty at Stanford University, Spring 1994.

---

[2] Used with the generous permission of the Stanford University News Service.

Aftermath

Hunger v. Integrity

'It has always seemed strange to me,' said Doc. 'The things we admire in men, kindness and generosity, openness, honesty, understanding and feeling are the concomitants of failure in our system. And those traits we detest, sharpness, greed, acquisitiveness, meanness, egotism and self-interest are the traits of success. And while men admire the quality of the first they love the produce of the second.'

'Who wants to be good if he has to be hungry too?' said Richard Frost.

John Steinbeck – *Cannery Row*

Losing My Self

☙

IN THE DAYS, months and years that followed my abrupt and angry resignation from the Stanford Law School, I lost my self. I didn't know who I was, where I was going, or what I would do tomorrow. On some days I felt a sense of overwhelming numbness. On others I experienced a grinding psychic pain. I became unable to focus on the details of my life. Simple tasks like taking out the garbage, preparing meals, or writing a check became unmanageable. I experienced overwhelming fatigue. When I slept I dreamt of anxiety and loss and woke up feeling exhausted. I was easily provoked into raging arguments and fights over mundane matters. I became hypersensitive to lies. I desperately needed to be around people I could count on to always tell the truth, people who wouldn't try to distort what I knew was real. I could not talk about the hell I had been cast into without great pain, explosive anger, and abundant tears. So I became silent. In short, I felt like I was more than slightly mad.

The anxiety manifested itself in a variety of ways. Sometimes it felt like an anchor on my heart. At other times it felt like a fever in my chest. My breathing would always become constricted. I couldn't take full, deep breaths, only shallow desperate gasps that left me worn out and starved for air. I remember being so full of dread at one point I thought my head and chest would explode, splattering the walls with gray brain matter and pink lung tissue and blood.

My head was always full of noise. It was as if there was a radio implanted in my brain. And it only had one station and that station had only one program – a twenty-four hour talk show where all of the conversation was about me. Me interviewing me about me, me interviewing others about me, others interviewing me and others about me. And I couldn't switch it off or turn down the volume.

It didn't take much – an offhand remark in a conversation, a sentence in a text, an image on a television or movie screen – to send me spiraling into a fit of anxiety, volcanic anger, or acute sadness. One night, as I lay curled up in a fetal position on the sofa in the den I became so angry watching Ken Starr being interviewed by Larry King I felt as if had suddenly come down with a stomach wrenching virus. King was talking to Starr about his recent decision to resign as special prosecutor in the Whitewater investigation. *"Here is one of the most hated figures of the late 20ᵗʰ century American political scene,"* I explained to the interviewer in my head. *"The man who tried to destroy a president because he disagreed with his politics and was envious of his sex life. The man who tried to bring down a government the people said they wanted to remain in place. The man who was viewed as a clown and an idiot by people the world over. Here he is calm, smooth and confident – being interviewed on national television like he's some rock star."*

Starr told King that the views people had of him did not trouble him. "It was simply about legal right and wrong – about enforcing the law. Crimes had been committed and I was charged with investigating the matter and bringing the culprit to justice," he said smugly.

I bolted up off the sofa, threw off the security blanket that was obviously failing me, and screamed at the flickering television screen: *"Where in the hell is your sense of perspective! Prosecutors make choices based on the context, the severity of the crime, resources constraint, compassion, and concern for the greater social good. Are you so without sin that you can cast stones at all the rest of us! Who in the hell appointed you? – God!"*

Starr said that it had never occurred to him to curtail the scope of the investigation even as the costs mounted and the foundations of the republic shook. *"You spent $47 million dollars of my money, asshole! Couldn't you have found a better use for it? I mean children in America go to school and to bed hungry. Millions of Americans can't read! Hello?"*

Starr's demeanor suggested that he believed he had behaved like the consummate, disinterested, honorable judge and legal professional. He must have used the word "professional" a hundred times during the interview. His face betrayed no anguish or discomfort. He wore a beatific smirk and the self-satisfied, look of innocence. He gave no hint that his agenda was anything but the pursuit of justice and the faithful execution of his "professional" responsibilities. I wanted to obliterate his face, which made me hate the person I had become. It felt as though I inhabited an alien body, as though I was going through the motions of someone else's life.

One morning not long after the Ken Starr episode, I woke up crying – something I hardly ever allowed myself to do because I was afraid that once the tears started flowing they would never stop, that maybe I would go on crying for another 400 years. My mind would not let go of an image I had seen the night before in a documentary[xlii] about black steelworkers that had aired on PBS.

The film focused on stories told by black men, and a few women, about the struggle for equal opportunity in U.S. steel mills. The people featured were mostly in their 70s. They had rough dark brown faces and spoke with unadorned dignity.

One man in particular talked about how he had come to be a crane operator. As he spoke, his eyes rolled upward and moved rapidly from side to side as if he was watching a scene from a film playing in the top of his head. He recalled with obvious joy how he was drawn to the crane operators perched high above the plant, drawn by the grace of their deft, coordinated movements. And he knew immediately that was the job he wanted to do. He was so drawn to the dance of the cranes that he would arrive at work an hour early to watch them. The crane jobs were good jobs and, like all the good jobs at the plant, were reserved for whites. He nevertheless mustered enough courage one day to ask the manger if he could be a crane operator. The manager told him that there were no openings. He kept going back day after day and each time he got the same response. When he told the manager that he had seen new faces on the cranes, the manager told him he was mistaken. Then one morning he was invited to give it a try. New men were always given a training session before being sent to operate a crane but he was sent in without so much as a minute of instruction. At the memory of that slight he began to cry and seemed taken aback that it was so still so painful to recall. The tears spilled down his face as he tried in vain to wipe them away with his thick, callused hands. He went on to tell how he triumphed in that moment. He said he knew instinctively what to do because unbeknownst to him, as he had watched the cranes with awe and hope over a period of almost two years, he had actually absorbed a lesson in their use.

He wept again when he recalled that he had eventually become one of the best crane operators at the plant. He said it once, and then he said it again, as if surprised by the magnitude of his own achievement. And as if to make sure that the world would also know what he had done, he said it again and when he said it that last time his shoulders straightened and he stopped crying.

I woke up crying that morning because I knew exactly what he meant and exactly what he felt even though thousands had marched and sat and laid their bodies down in protest so that I wouldn't have to know that kind of pain.

I could not do anything cerebral. I mostly avoided my home office. I could not function there. I moved papers from one side of my L-shaped desk to the other – some for more than a year. I would spend hours staring at the growing mounds of paper in a panic. On my better days I would pick up one of the papers and be able to get as far as deciding what my choices were about what should be done with it – respond, toss it, file it. But I had so little confidence in my judgment that I couldn't make a choice or follow it through. I might decide that it needed to be filed but where? Under what label? With what other papers? If I decided it needed a response, I couldn't even begin to imagine what it should be. And I couldn't throw anything away.

I ate constantly – almost every hour on the hour. I didn't allow myself to ever feel hungry – not even for a minute. My mouth was constantly in motion, chomping down on some morsel of something or other desperately seeking comfort in that fleeting sensual pleasure like a sex addict.

As the months wore on, I awoke earlier and earlier – 4:00 AM, 3:00 A.M., 2:00 A.M., 1:00 A.M. I would usually wake up in a sweat – hot and thirsty, my pajamas clinging to my damp skin. I was having fitful, disturbing dreams although on waking I could rarely remember the details or even the broad story outline. I had to struggle just to remember who I was. I couldn't even recall what it felt like to be me.

I couldn't bring myself to get up when it was still dark. It felt too dangerous. So I would lie in bed until the sun came up – listening to the radio in my head. *"Don't you you know that chronic sleep deprivation is hazardous to you health?"* the interviewer says to me accusingly. *"The experts say it results in diminished mental acuity, shortened tempers, and a tendency to doze at every quiet moment. It also causes marked alterations in metabolic and endocrine function. When is the last time you had a good night's sleep?"*

I actually can't remember ever feeling fully rested. In my first two years at Stanford I pulled all-nighters before almost every class – that would be at least three times a week. I did a lot of all-nighters when I was in private practice too. But I was moving in a world that practically placed a moral value on sleeping as little as possible. All-nighters were seen as a badge of honor, as evidence of toughness, of commitment to the insitution and the profession. To admit to needing sleep, was seen as an emblem of weakness, of laziness, of lack of will and discipline.

When morning finally came, I was so paralyzed by doubt I couldn't decide what to do. Should I stay in bed and play my medidation tape? Should I listen to NPR's Morning Edition? Should I invite the dog to join me in a snuggle? Should I warm myself against my husband and let the firmness of his body and his breathing steady me before I tried to face the day?

Usually the need to go to the bathroom would get me moving. But before I reached it I would again be paralyzed by indecision. Should I pick up the New York Times before or after? Most mornings, I rushed to the front door to get the paper first even though I knew I would be better off if I didn't read it. Invariably there would be some story about some injustice somewhere in the world.

I would scurry back to my cavernous, white tiled sanctuary with the newspaper tucked under my arm, turn on the space heater, and plunk myself down on the toilet. I would scour the pages of the newspaper for glimpses of other people's lives. Sometimes I would stumble on personal success stories and I knew it would be a bad day, especially if the story was about a woman or a person of color or, God forbid, a black woman around my age. *"Don't these stories prove that racism and sexism are not obstacles to success?"* the interviewer in my head would posit smugly. *"I suppose,"* my mind would answer meekly. *"I guess if I had been smart and focused and hardworking I too would be a CEO, a Dean, an established author..."* Invariably I ended up in the obituary section of the newspaper, losing myself in those elegant recitations of the journey of some notable soul. I was looking for evidence that things could turn around in a life gone awry, that people overcame failures, that they found their way to new and better places before they came to the end of their days.

In the Spring of 1999, Dieter and I rented our Palo Alto house filled with all of our possessions and fled to Italy with our dog, Kai, a mutt of unknown origin. We settled in a two-room dwelling at *I Cappuccini*, a 15th century monastery converted into modest vacation apartments nestled in the hills above Passignano, a small Umbrian village on the shores of Lago Trasimeno.

Passignano is a place so ancient that the immediate past lost some of its suffocating power. It fulfilled the overwhelming desire that had seized me in the aftermath of my Stanford tragedy for a rural life of isolation and reflection, worlds away from the madness of Silicon Valley. I needed to be in a place where my daily life would have a dependable rhythm and a natural, unchanging landscape. I needed to be in an enclosed, encompassable, safe space.

I was looking for refuge from a land that treated me like an unwelcome stranger even though my roots there ran deeper than those of many who disdained me. Passignano wasn't my home and Italy wasn't my country, so there would be no cost to not belonging to that place. I wouldn't be plagued by the shame or longing I felt as an expatriate in my own homeland.

In my new simplified existence at *I Cappuccini*, I found solace in the non-mechanized performance of ordinary household chores – the very activities that education, feminism, technology, and money were supposed to free me from: hand washing dishes in warm, soapy, sloppy water; sweeping cool tiled floors with a broom; toasting bread on a stovetop in a pan; hanging clothes out on a line to dry in the sun and wallowing in their freshness when I retrieved them at day's end; walking daily down the same winding mountain road to the local village to buy food for our evening meal and slowly but surely forging connections with the people I encountered along the way.

Cooking and cleaning set the pace and tone of my new life. It established a certain rhythm – a slow, monotonous, reliable beat, like the sound and motion of a train. That tempo carried me through each day, assuring me that I was moving toward some destination and that I would arrive safely and on time.

Admittedly, I would not have viewed these chores as restorative if I had had to perform them under time pressure; if I had had a brood of children; if I had not enjoyed a sense of noble sacrifice in their doing because I could have hired someone to do them for me.

All of my work was now unpaid. [Linda tutored several times a week in an East Palo Alto literacy program. Later she became a part-time administrator in an affordable housing non-profit.]^{xliii} And yet I found in my work a joy I had not known in twenty years. The regularity, simplicity, and honesty of these activities comforted me. I got immediate results that you could see, and touch, and smell, which gave me a firm sense of accomplishment that was so often lacking in my paid work. And those results could be judged by objective standards and were subject to no judgment but my own.

When we finally came home to California, household chores continued to be the focus of my life. And I found that it changed the way I inhabited my house. The bedroom, the bathrooms, the garden, and, most of all, the kitchen became my principal domains. My home office went un-entered and untouched for more than two years. It also changed the way I inhabited the world outside my home. I became a regular visitor at the local supermarket, scouring the aisles for the more exotic items like golden tomatoes, smoked trout, and fennel that my new, creative recipes demanded. We now ate with the seasons because I had the time to notice what season we were in and what fruits and vegetables it produced.

MY FAMILY WAS A LIE

I FIRST LEARNED that my family was a lie just a few weeks into the new millennium. I read and re-read that e-mail so many times that even today I can recite it nearly word for word. It said, "I am looking for answers to pressing questions I have had since my adolescence. You see, we have the same biological father."

Bryan Glynn set forth a brief, elegant synopsis of his life, starting with his birth in 1964 to a young woman named Audrey who was a nurse at Harlem hospital where my father was a resident. He told of his visits to Dr. Mabry's office in Manhattan and of being sent off to military school at my father's suggestion and with his financial assistance. While there he befriended the only other black boy at the school, a boy named Michael Boyde – whom, he later learned, was also Dr. Mabry's son. He joined the National Guard and later the army reserves, graduated from university, then married his college sweetheart and settled down in suburban Washington, D.C. with his wife and two daughters, just twenty minutes, it turned out, from where my brother Ralph [Tommy] lived with his wife and two sons.

Bryan said that my father had "skirted" his responsibilities to him and his mother but that he bore my father no ill will. "My life," he wrote, "has not actually been a tragedy, but there is a hole," that he hoped we could help fill by telling him some things about the father he had barely known.

When I finally met him in person, I saw that he was unmistakably my father's son. His triangular head and narrow mustache and that gap in his front teeth were achingly familiar. I was so overwhelmed I had trouble hearing and making sense of the words that spilled from his mouth. Bryan is calm, grounded, and directed. He speaks with a quiet honesty and listens attentively.

I told Bryan what little I knew about my father's origins and past, that he had been raised by his maternal grandparents in Valdosta, Georgia. He, too, had been born out of wedlock and his father had rejected both him and his mother and refused to support or even acknowledge them. His

101

mother had left him in the care of her parents and moved to New York. My great-grandfather was a Choctaw Indian and his wife was a deeply religious African American woman so fair she could have passed for white. I had been told that my great grandmother was so determined to see my father succeed in school, that she supervised his homework closely and would beat his head bloody with a wooden spoon when he made a mistake. She died suddenly when my father was about thirteen during a trip to New York, where she had taken him for a rare visit to his mother. My father never returned to Valdosta but was instead left in the care of his mother, who now had seven other children and an alcoholic husband, who promptly banished him to an unfinished attic room in their Brooklyn brownstone. In spite of these circumstances, my father went on to become the first in his family to graduate from high school and topped even that by earning a medical degree from the Université Libre de Bruxelles.

I told Bryan that even though I had grown up in my father's household, I did not know him well as a person. He has always been an enigmatic stranger to me. I cannot recall ever having had a real conversation with my father. He has rarely spoken to me. When he has, he's always talked at – and never with – me. And all he's ever talked about is himself – his battles and his triumphs – or impersonal matters like national or international politics. Nevertheless, I have always sensed that deep inside him there is an abiding sadness.

I was grateful, I told Bryan, that my father stayed and supported and raised us even though he could have chosen to leave. I was grateful for the education he had pushed me to pursue and sacrificed enormously to pay for. I regretted that he seemed unable to take any joy in my eventual success or to give me any credit for my contributions to that success or to his life. I regretted most of all that he had not seen fit to give Bryan the same advantages I had enjoyed.

Bryan insisted, several times, that he had not had a deprived childhood, and that his mother had raised and cared for him well. His mother was married when Bryan was born and although the marriage ended not long afterward, he considered that man – whose last name he bears – to be his father. Mr. Glynn was not greatly involved in Bryan's life but Bryan said that whenever he called him for something, he could always count on Mr. Glynn to deliver. By implication, my father could not, it seems, be similarly counted on.

Bryan also insisted several times that he was not bitter or angry. He was grateful for my father's intervention in sending him to military school when he started "acting up" and giving his mother a hard time. That experience turned his life around, he said. He credits that time with much of his current success. He said he had not seen my father in over twenty years. He last spoke to him in 1991 when his army reserve unit was about to deploy to Saudi Arabia to fight in the [First] Gulf War. My father, true to form, had launched into a political diatribe against the war when the humane thing to do would have been to express concern and compassion for his son.

As I listened to Bryan talk about his own life, it became clear that his resemblance to my father is only physical. Bryan is sensitive about the needs of his family in ways my father never was. He cherishes his two daughters whom he appears to know far better than my father has ever known my sister or me. He remains loyal to his wife and supportive of her needs and interests. He had just been given a promotion requiring him to move his family from the suburbs of Washington, D.C. to Delaware and he seemed to have given a great deal of thought to how this move would affect his wife's career and his daughters' connections to school, friends and community.

Meeting Bryan made me reassess our family's relationships with other women. Chief among these women was Christine, a lovely, immaculately coifed, stylishly dressed young blonde who became a friend of the family and developed a particular fondness for me. I don't know how Christine came into our lives, but it now occurs to me that she may well have been one of my father's mistresses. I don't think Christine lived in our neighborhood. She would appear at our house as if out of nowhere, like a fairy, dressed in tailored suits and dresses and stockings and spike heels, smelling like a delicately scented flower and bearing small gifts for the children. She brought lightness and laughter to our home and I loved her.

THE TRIAL I DIDN'T HAVE

❦

I WAS DRIVEN to stand up and walk noisily out of Stanford by an instinct for survival. In the immediate aftermath my life, which up until that point had been guided almost solely by my intellect, went into a tailspin. At that time, mutual friends in Palo Alto introduced me to Colleen Crangle[xliv], a woman who had already filed a discrimination lawsuit against Stanford University and formed a coalition with other women. Having grown up in Zimbabwe and South Africa as both a white and a woman, Colleen was especially sensitive to issues of race and gender equity and understood my Stanford experience.

Connecting with Colleen stabilized me. By her own example she enabled me to see that what I had done was not some irrational, insane act but justified and meaningful.

A brilliant woman with a PhD in Philosophy and a graduate degree in Computer Science, Colleen had been a Senior Research Scientist in the bioinformatics lab at the Stanford School of Medicine. The year before my departure she had brought suit against the university's discriminatory practices and the case was finally coming to trial. This would be the first discrimination case against Stanford to ever go to trial.

I didn't miss a single day of the proceedings. I went so I could be there for Colleen. I also went because I desperately needed to be there for me. My own case had not gone to trial and I lamented having missed the chance to air my grievances in open court, even though I knew I might have collapsed from the attack on my competence and worth the University planned to use as its main line of defense.

In many ways Colleen's story was all of our stories. Except for the fact that I had resigned and Colleen was fired, the essential facts of her case were distressingly similar. She was let go on one day's notice by Edward Shortliffe,[xlv] an associate dean with the bioinformatics lab, for daring to challenge an attempt to demote her to a subordinate position simply because a male colleague had found her to be "a threat." In a lab that had never seen a woman on its senior research staff, her assuming a leadership role, she had been told, would be like "the tail wagging the dog."

I had high hopes for Colleen's trial. I wanted her to win, of course, and believed she would prevail and score one for us against the University. But more than that, I wanted 'our' story to be told – one demeaning, spirit-killing remark at a time, one marginalizing act of omission at a time, one career-derailing act of repression at a time. I wanted the world to catch a glimpse of the real lives of some of the women whose presence at institutions like Stanford is so often pointed to as evidence that the glass ceiling has been shattered.

My faith that Colleen would succeed – that she would be heard and believed and that the jury would rule in her favor – was far more than I could ever have felt about my own aborted case. Although at core our Stanford dramas were nearly identical, there was one crucial difference of Colleen being white. Winning meant overcoming the defense that it was somehow all your fault – that you weren't good enough to be there. I thought a white woman had a better chance to defeat this line of argument. She would elicit empathy I could never get. She could be their mother, sister, wife, or daughter. People, even blacks, have a hard time feeling empathy for blacks. I believed that jurors and others hearing a white woman's story would less readily accept the defense customarily advanced in these cases: that the person claiming discrimination was incompetent and simply not good enough to be at the institution, someone whose demotion, lack of promotion, or firing was justified and, indeed, necessary if the institution were to protect its high standards of excellence.

My intuitive sense of this had been confirmed in the first weeks following my resignation from Stanford. A former colleague of mine in law practice, a white man with whom my husband and I regularly socialized, heard that other women on the Stanford faculty had come forward with claims of discrimination. If it had been just black people, he said, you would have to seriously consider the possibility that it wasn't discrimination, they simply weren't qualified. But you can't say that about all those women. The white man's wife, who is Lebanese, told me this without realizing what she was revealing about the man she shared her life with.

I should have been devastated by that remark. But I was already so numb from the character assaults launched at me behind my back as I made my way out of the University, so battle-hardened from struggling to stand my ground, that I responded strategically rather than emotionally. I decided at that moment to hitch myself to the wagon of those pioneering white Stanford women like Colleen. By standing in the compassionate light in which I believed their stories would be seen, I could perhaps get the world to see that I too had suffered an injustice.

I had known Colleen for slightly less than a year by the time her case went to trial. We had first connected not through Stanford or academic circles but through the community of Palo Alto school moms. Elspeth

Farmer, the Visiting Scholar at the Law School in my last year there, had young children who attended Duveneck, the same Palo Alto school as Colleen's children. Word had spread rapidly through the informal network of Duveneck moms that Colleen was suing Stanford for gender discrimination. I imagine that Colleen's action stirred something buried deep in those women, many of whom are highly educated over-achievers whose marriages to high-earning men enabled them to choose to abandon their careers as lawyers and business executives to become stay-at-home moms. While the conflicting demands of high-powered professional jobs and family no doubt contributed to their decision to opt for stay-at-home motherhood, I suspect that many did not so much choose to retreat to their kitchens and family rooms as they were driven there by the male-oriented culture of the places where they once worked – a culture that demands loyalty to the organization above all else that is demonstrated principally by inordinate amounts of face time, much of it unproductive; a culture that emphasizes showy demonstrations of prowess over quiet efficiency, and confrontation over collaboration.

It was through Colleen that I connected with other Stanford faculty women who were battling the University and whom I would join in an unprecedented collective legal challenge to the University under federal equal opportunity laws through the U.S. Department of Labor.[xlvi] In all of my professional life I had never had the experience of talking openly with other women about the humiliations, the frustrations, the pain and the anger we experienced. Nor had I ever had the experience of women standing up for each other and standing together. A group of us met regularly, calling ourselves the Stanford Seven. We quickly developed the kind of bond I imagine forms between the members of a small battalion in the midst of war.

On the days I went to court I was punctual and paid a great deal of attention to what I wore, something I had not done in the months since I had left the University. I needed to be comfortable but I also wanted to be dignified, so I chose outfits that were casual but elegant. I wore muted colors and studiously avoided black out of fear that wearing funereal colors might doom the outcome. It's funny how superstitious you can become when faced with dangerous situations over which you have no control. I wore my most stylish low-heeled European pumps, without stockings. I put on foundation and powder and blush for the first time in months. I even put on lipstick.

I always sat in the same place in the courtroom – in the corner on the last row of benches on plaintiff's side. It felt like a safe space and it had a good view. Few would notice me but I could see the whole tableau – the judge, the jury, the plaintiff, the defendants, the lawyers, and the observers who had come to watch this drama unfold.

On the day that Colleen testified, I arrived at the courthouse earlier and looked better than on any other day. The spectator gallery quickly filled and the air inside the courtroom was soon hot, heavy, and suffocating under harsh fluorescent light.

Stanford's supporters sat on the right behind a phalanx of more than half a dozen high-priced lawyers. Stanford's principal trial lawyers, Michael Lucey and Greta Schnetzler, sat at counsel's table. Lucey and Schnetzler had successfully petitioned the judge to allow Ted Shortliffe to join them at counsel's table after he had testified and been cross-examined, under the pretext that they needed him to assist them during the proceedings. But I believed they wanted him to be there in the hopes that it would unsettle Colleen. The rest of Stanford's legal team sat with a group of university officials behind a partition separating spectators from those officially involved in the proceedings. From my vantage point on the far left of the gallery, I could see only the backs of the Stanford contingent. They all wore suits of gray and black, women and men alike, and their shoulders drooped forward as if the lies that filled them prevented them from standing erect.

Colleen's supporters filled the benches between me and the partition behind the counsel's table manned by Colleen and her two lawyers, Dan Siegal and Ann Weills. They were almost all women, some quite advanced in years, attired in varied styles of multicolored dress.

As Dan Siegal, Colleen's principal trial lawyer, led her through her testimony, I grabbed each of Colleen's words like a drowning person reaching for a lifeline even though I knew her story so well I could have testified in her place. When Siegal asked her to tell the jury how everything that had happened made her feel, I lost my battle to stay afloat.

"I find it difficult to talk about because it's very shaming for me. I have such a wonderful education and wonderful gifts and I really would like to be using them for good."

"I trusted the people I worked with and I don't like to admit it but I feel afraid about working in situations like that again. It's as if you are driving in a car and someone you trust comes alongside and swipes you off the road and there's a terrible accident and then you have to get back onto the road again and drive and it just feels terrifying."

In that moment Denise [Johnson[xlvii]] and Jessica [Rose Agramonte [xlviii]], two of the other Stanford women who had challenged the university on race and gender equity, turned to look at me. They wore identical masks of sorrow. When I refocused my gaze on the front of the courtroom, the benches holding all those women became church pews holding mourners, the witness box a coffin, the judge a preacher, and the jury a choir.

When Michael Lucey, Stanford's principal lawyer, rose to begin the cross-examination I braced myself for an onslaught. I thought about leaving but I couldn't move. I closed my eyes and breathed slowly and deeply in a futile effort to relieve the pressure in my chest.

Lucey was immediately hostile and aggressive, positing bogus charges that Colleen had to put to rest. Lucey then went on to challenge Colleen's qualifications to be considered the equal of the male colleagues who felt so threatened by her presence, also without success. His final tactic was to attack her credibility by challenging her account of conversations that, as she had told them, revealed so clearly and convincingly the extent of his clients' hostility toward their lone female colleague. He loaded his dart gun with the preposterous lies these men had concocted in their defense and fired.

Isn't it true, he asked, that Dr. Fagan[xlix] was simply trying to help you when you asked for help? Larry Fagan was the colleague whose protestations and machinations instigated Colleen's demotion and ultimately her dismissal. As Lucey spun his web of lies and facile rationalizations, his voice smooth, seductive and full of irony, I grabbed the edge of the bench with both hands to steady myself. I was afraid I would pass out.

Colleen took Lucey head on. She avoided his poisonous darts with skill and grace and sometimes even threw them back at him. And every time she did he would reach behind his back and manipulate and twist his pen in his clenched hand as if it were her neck.

Lucey had a female co-counsel, Greta Schnetzler, who sat with him at counsel's table but addressed the court on only a handful of occasions when she was allowed to lead the questioning of a few minor witnesses. When Greta walked past the small group of Stanford women gathered in the narrow hallway outside the courtroom during recesses, she looked past us, her eyes desperately searching for some inanimate object of significance to focus on. Her gait, which in the courtroom had projected forced determination, became stiff and awkward – as if she couldn't quite remember how to walk – and her face turned stony white. By the end of the trial I felt so sorry for Greta I would sometimes smile at her when she walked past me. Even though mine was a weak, unenthusiastic smile with a hint of condescension, Greta would offer a hesitant, apologetic smile with a hint of gratitude in reply.

I was confident the jury would rule in Colleen's favor, even though Stanford's defense had closed asking, "So has everybody lied?" "If you accept Dr. Crangle's statement of the facts," Lucey said," you have to assume everybody who got on the stand … lied to you, lied under oath. Now is that reasonable to assume?"

The jury deliberated for less than six hours. We stood by at home, waiting to be summoned to the courthouse. Once there, we gathered in a small anteroom, barely large enough to hold us: Colleen, her two lawyers, her husband and me. I remember walking in and cheerily announcing, "This is a good day for a victory." The tension in their faces dissipated long enough to allow a smile. Colleen, whose faith had carried her to that day, had her bible open to a favorite verse: *Truly my soul silently waits for God: From Him comes my salvation. He only is my rock and my salvation; He is my defense; I shall not be greatly moved*.

The uniformed court officer knocked and leaned into the room "They're coming in," he said, instantly silencing the chatter we had filled the room with in an effort to crowd out the fear.

The courtroom was largely empty. None of the Stanford supporters were there. On that day in March 2000, the jurors found unanimously in Colleen's favor on all matters put before them. They awarded the maximum amount allowed under federal law for punitive and compensatory damages, finding that she had made a good faith claim of sex discrimination and that, in response, her employers had retaliated against her, acting with malice, or a reckless disregard to her protected rights.

That night we gathered at Colleen's house. As we celebrated her victory, I realized why this meant so much to me. Colleen's trial was the trial I never had.

Victory party at Colleen's house, March 31, 2000. Karen Sawislik, Colleen, Jessica Rose-Agramonte, and Linda.

AM I STILL SOMEBODY?

❧

ON A CHILLY DAY in 2000, Bill Gould[ii], my former Stanford colleague, called to invite my husband, Dieter, and me to his home for dinner. It was an unexpected and not especially welcome invitation but one that I felt obliged to accept. Bill lived in the "faculty ghetto" on the Stanford campus, a collection of mostly older homes whose million dollar price tags put them well beyond the reach of younger faculty. I had not been on campus since that warm spring day in 1999 when I followed the last box out of my office and drove home behind the moving truck packed with the remains of a quarter century of my life.

Bill was then the only tenured African American at the law school. He didn't say why he had decided to invite us and I thought it would be impolite to ask. In all my years on the faculty Bill had never so much as invited me to have a cup of coffee with him. Despite his enormous accomplishments – he is a world-renowned labor lawyer and arbitrator, has authored more books by far than anyone else on the faculty, and served as Chairman of the National Labor Relations Board under President Clinton – he is essentially invisible to his colleagues. Their inability to see him caused him to literally disappear. Sightings of Bill at the law school were rare. He didn't even bother to attend faculty meetings; one of the few things professors are required to do that is generally observed and enforced.

Bill surfaced briefly to take a stand on my behalf in the controversy that ultimately led me to resign. That was the only time in seven years I was in Bill's office. It was overrun with books and papers that lay piled on every available surface, including most of the floor. Framed photos of Bill and various public figures – like Ted Kennedy and Nelson Mandela and several U.S. Presidents – as well as plaques honoring Bill for some accomplishment or other hung lopsided on the walls or sat tucked into corners of the overstuffed floor to ceiling bookcase that lined the back wall, or perched on top of a pile of reading material.

The evening of the dinner I dressed in black – a flowing, ankle length black wool dress, black tights, and flat black shoes that would allow my feet to remain firmly planted on the ground. We loaded Dieter's wheelchair and the portable ramp into the van and drove slowly out of our sheltering cul-de-sac.

I took a deep breath as we turned into Campus Drive, and peered through the darkness searching for landmarks of my past. When we drove past the rear of the law school buildings, my body stiffened, recalling the suffocating anxiety that had gripped me on mornings I had to teach.

As we pulled up in front of Bill's house the gnawing sense of being off-center that had haunted me during all my years as an academic descended upon me and settled in my core. I carried the portable ramp up to the threshold and quietly put it in place. When we had successfully maneuvered the wheelchair onto the landing, Dieter adjusted his legs so that his feet were stationed firmly on the footrests. I smoothed my skirt and knocked on the door.

We heard the sound of heavy feet moving briskly toward the front of the house and the door swung open. Bill hadn't changed. He had the same slightly dazed but enthusiastic manner. He wore a jacket and tie, which made him look like a figure from the 1950s and out of place even in his own house. Bill greeted us warmly and introduced us to his Anne, his English wife, who came up behind him as we stepped into the front hall. As they led us into the living room I heard the chatter of other voices and realized that we were not the only guests.

I stood in stunned silence and disbelief when I realized that Bill had invited another member of the law school faculty. Hank Greely[lii] occupied one end of the sofa and a woman, whom I learned was his wife, sat on the other. The third couple, whom I didn't know, an Asian man from Oakland and his wife, who was white, sat in armchairs opposite the sofa. He was a journalist whom we learned in the course of the evening was recovering from colon cancer, although we never learned what his relationship to Bill and Anne was.

I couldn't figure out why Bill had brought this motley assortment of guests together. It turned out that none of the assembled guests was close either to the hosts or to each other. How could Bill not have known that I would be uncomfortable spending an evening in Hank Greely's presence? Hank Greely – with whom I'd had no meaningful interaction in my entire time at the law school, and whose publication record did not seem to me to justify his award of tenure – had come to embody everything that made me choose to leave.

As Greely slid over toward his wife, I squeezed onto the far end of the sofa, leaning into the armrest, to avoid touching him. I didn't look into Greely's face once the whole evening. "Happy New Year. Nice to see you," he said without extending his hand, an omission for which I was enormously grateful. Nothing was ever said then or the rest of the evening about my having been at Stanford Law School or having left. No one ever inquired about how or what I was doing. I was almost totally silent and was grateful to Dieter for his charm and his loquaciousness. I felt like the reluctant, accompanying spouse.

The evening's conversation was entirely about two subjects. The presidential campaign and HMOs, with a word or two from Dieter about the German electoral process and social welfare system. Mrs. Dr. Greely went on for more than an hour singing the praises of the Kaiser system where she had her lung practice. She argued for more statistics-based medical care. I asked her about the unquantifiable, but in my experience, powerfully important effect of a strong personal relationship between physician and patient, saying, "I read an article in the Sunday Times recently about the placebo effect, about the curative power of a gesture, or a word of sympathy or hope from a caring, trusted physician." Mrs. Dr. Greely dismissed that as "romanticizing."

I wasn't angry. I was more incredulous, bored and slightly amused. But I also felt like I was being tested, being pressured to show how smart and incisive I could be. I had to remind myself that I was gone from that world and that what they thought of me no longer mattered.

Since then I rarely tell anyone that I used to be a lawyer – a partner in a prestigious San Francisco firm – and almost never mention that I used to be a professor at Stanford Law School. But I think about having been a lawyer and a law professor nearly every single day.

I think about it every morning when I settle down on the faded brown leather saddle of my fancy English city bike and pedal out the driveway toward my part-time administrator's job at the small affordable housing non-profit by the railroad tracks that lie in Stanford's shadow. I remember how seldom I rode my bicycle to the law school despite having paid over $1,000 for it on a whim because I liked the delicate garden green frame, and the skirt guard, and the sturdy wicker basket strung on the front handle bars, and the fact that it was English. I thought it would distinguish me – make it look like I belonged in Palo Alto and at Stanford. These days a thousand dollars is half a month's pay. If I needed a new bicycle I would prowl the garage sales. But these days I ride to work nearly every single day because I am rarely pressed for time and I start my days well rested and I don't leave the house heavy with dread and too many casebooks.

I think about it every time I opt to cook instead of eating out, which is nearly every night. I've learned to duplicate many of the dishes we favored in the local restaurants we frequented three, sometimes four times a week because I couldn't find the time to get to the supermarket and, even when I did, was too exhausted to cook food I bought without much thought or pleasure. These days I'm in Whole Foods three or four times a week, marveling at the sight and feel and smell of the abundant fresh organic produce – examining with a cook's eye and a childlike fascination the cool, smooth, taut deep purple skin of the eggplants; breathing in the pungent freshness of sun-colored citrus fruits like a wine connoisseur at a tasting; imagining oyster mushrooms as some fantastical creature born in the woods but raised in the sea. And cooking has become a joy instead of a chore.

"I'm not a lawyer, but..."I've said without a trace of irony or shame on a number of occasions. I've used plain English so as not to betray my secret.

The other day I lied. I told someone I was a Stanford Law Professor. I said it with anger and determination. I practically shoved it down her throat. It was a defensive move.

The tangible evidence of my past life as a lawyer and a law professor lay crammed for some time in green and white file boxes, stacked precariously, six high and two deep against the longest wall of my garage. By the time I got around to carrying them to the city dump, the spiders and the silverfish were far more familiar with their contents than the dazed and angry woman who had packed them.

In Palo Alto I rarely see anyone who looks like me. One day Dieter was sitting in his electric blue wheelchair chatting with the slim brown-skinned girl with long straightened hair who works as a nanny for our next-door neighbors. She smiled broadly as I alighted from the car, walked toward me with the baby balanced on her hip and in a tone full of levity and cordiality said, "I didn't know you were his wife. I thought you were his attendant."

In my parents' quest to open up our world, we lost something. We lost a sense of being rooted. An opportunity to see ourselves reflected back. A chance to live in a place where we were not constantly reminded of being different, of being less.

I am a child of the dream[liii]. And I am ashamed to admit that I have been living a nightmare. It isn't what they sought to give us. But it is what we got. We are caught in limbo – halfway between a world of us and them.

Of course, maybe what I feel has nothing to do with race, but is merely a function of being human at a time of great uncertainty. Maybe it's just what everyone feels on turning fifty, when maybe more lies behind than ahead. That is the tragedy of racism: that you doubt what you feel is a simple human yearning because you live in a culture that constantly denies your full humanity.

When I was growing up in Harlem in the 1960s I dreamt obsessively of being someone who mattered and living in a place that was pretty and safe. Palo Alto, California – where houses cost more per square foot than in any other city in America – is both pretty and safe. My marriage to my German husband, Dieter, fulfilled my desire to be loved. He didn't fit any of the images I had built up for myself over the years about my ideal mate. I'm sure he's not what my father had in mind, but this choice turned out to be the best decision I ever made. Dieter, an engineer ten years my senior, had been forced to retire from the high tech world where he achieved professional and financial success. Multiple sclerosis had crippled his legs but left his spirit untouched. My love and my rock, he was the first person I let see the real me. I realized I did not have to be a Stanford law professor or law firm partner to be somebody who matters. It doesn't matter what other people think. In the end, the only thing that matters is the quality of the human connections that you have made.

HOUSE OF HEALING FIRE

❧

IN THE AFTERMATH and subsequent loss of my professional life, I decided in 2000 to return to the place where my American journey began: Harlem and the house at Two-Sixty-Two. My parents had never sold the house, they simply abandoned it and moved west. It had been empty for more than two decades. In the years since, Two-Sixty-Two became the dark, ugly secret no one in the family talked about, especially around my father who would become either morose or enraged at the mere mention of the place. I think it was because the memory of our years in that house held so much pain.

So in my 49th year I went back to Harlem because I thought that if I could fix the house on Strivers' Row, I could fix my broken life and heal my broken family.

I had visions of the Mabry clan gathered on the stoop of our restored brownstone, posing for a photo *à la* "A Great Day in Harlem," the famous 1958 photograph[liv] of renowned black jazz musicians spilling down onto the sidewalk from the steps of a house much like ours, looking easy, sassy, and proud. I flew to Las Vegas, Nevada, where my parents had moved on fleeing Harlem in the 1970s. Las Vegas had not brought my father the financial success he'd hoped to achieve. He had signed a deal with the Humana Corporation to open an office in a shiny new medical office building adjacent to one of their hospitals. The referrals Humana had promised to deliver never came. My father was the only black physician in the complex and the one to whom Humana referred all their indigent patients. With this clientele he couldn't bill enough to make his lease payments and the practice soon collapsed, leaving mountains of debt. As he neared his 70s my father went back to making house calls.

In Las Vegas I sat down in their living room, and dared to raise the question of Two-Sixty-Two. To my astonishment my father said, "Why don't you see what you can do?" I rushed to his den, typed-up a power-of-attorney giving me legal authority to manage the property in their name, and dragged him to a notary to sign it.

A Great Day In Harlem, 1958*. Musicians gathered on 126th Street, Harlem – including Count Basie, Art Blakey, Dizzy Gillespie, Coleman Hawkins, Charles Mingus, Thelonious Monk, Gerry Mulligan, Oscar Pettiford, Sonny Rollins and Lester Young.

My siblings and I were all estranged to some extent from my father, who seemed incapable of acknowledging or expressing joy or satisfaction about our achievements. At times he seemed almost jealous of our successes and contemptuous of the strength my sister and I demonstrated by taking charge of our lives and our families. Although we had more than fulfilled his obsessive desire that his children should be highly educated professionals by amassing an impressive collection of Ivy League degrees and rising to the top of our professions he still found plenty to criticize about the way we were conducting our lives. But he never once uttered a word of praise. I had been worried that he would find fault with my plan for the house and not support it.

Back home again in California I focused on the details of the trip to New York. My biggest concern was having to enter the house alone. So I tried to get at least one person from my immediate family to accompany me. I phoned my youngest brother Jerry, first. He is the most caring and responsive of my siblings. But this time Jerry never returned my calls. My older brother Tommy said he couldn't make it because he did not want to lose an entire working day. I didn't even bother asking my sister, Maggie.

---

* 'Harlem 1958' photo used with the generous permission of the Art Kane Archive, Pictures from a Revolutionary Artist.

We hadn't spoken in nearly two years. I never even considered asking my father. When my mother realized that I might have to go alone, she half-heartedly offered to join me but didn't protest when I suggested that perhaps she was too frail to make the trip. Indeed, she seemed grateful for the reprieve.

After my efforts to recruit a family member failed, I turned to strangers. Weeks of Internet research and phone calls produced a connection to one of Harlem's young developers – a man named Steve. Steve had impressive credentials. He was, among other things, one of the partners who owned the office complex on 125th Street where Bill Clinton had just decided to open his post-presidential headquarters.

I explained to Steve what I was trying to accomplish. I told him that I wanted to convert Two-Sixty-Two into a retirement asset for my parents. Even as a shell, Two-Sixty-Two was worth at least half a million dollars. By the early 1990s, Strivers' Row had become one of the most desirable blocks in a booming real estate market. I wanted to explore the possibility of using the equity to finance a renovation that could generate sufficient rental income to give my parents a financial cushion.

What I didn't say is that I wanted to take care of the house for its own sake. I wanted it to be whole, and warm, and safe, and beautiful. Moreover, I wanted to take care of me.

Steve agreed to meet me at the house and bring along a contractor who could help assess the damage I was sure awaited me. My parents had become so disconnected from Two-Sixty-Two they could no longer find the keys. So I arranged for a locksmith to be there as well.

The other thing I worried about when planning my trip was where I would stay. I had extended family in the New York area – an aunt and a myriad of cousins – but most I hardly knew, and those I did know evoked painful childhood memories and I didn't care to see them.

Harlem now had its own web page where I found two B & B's. Given the nature of my trip, the one called "The House of Healing Fire" had an irresistible cachet.

BACK TO HARLEM

❦

I FINALLY HEADED 'home' to Harlem in March 2001, traveling into a snowstorm that would blanket the East Coast. I tacked my journey onto a final professional junket, to Washington, D.C. to attend a daylong meeting of a special committee of the American Society of International Law (ASIL). The Society was the last remaining tie I had to my former life as a lawyer and law professor.

The meeting was held in a conference room at the office of a prominent law firm where the then President of the Society and Chair of the committee was a partner. The offices were much like those of the large firms I had practiced in – quiet, sleek, elegant, rich, imposing, intimidating.

We met in a mid-sized conference room, the kind that would be used for small meetings with colleagues or clients, or for ancillary negotiations during complex merger and acquisition transactions, or by a lone associate working late into the night who needed space to spread out the reams of paper a handshake between multinational conglomerates would generate. At the center of the room was a long custom mahogany conference table, whose intimidating heft was made less daunting by its high gloss finish. The table was surrounded by equally imposing dark blue leather armchairs, with thick but firm upholstery whose support lent stature to anyone occupying them. A long credenza, built to match the conference table and running almost the full length of the wall, held a paper doily-lined tray of fine French pastries, a coffee urn, sleek white china cups, saucers and dessert plates, and gleaming flatware.

Our task was to fill the position of Executive Director for the society. The applicants included the woman of color who was just completing her second successful term as the Society's Executive Director and wished to continue in the position. Over the course of the morning, the candidates we had pre-selected filed into the conference room. The committee consisted of four white men, including the committee chair, one white woman, and me. It came down to a choice between two candidates: the current

Executive Director and a white man who had held a prominent government job in the last days of the Clinton Administration. In his interview the man had expressed disdain for the administrative responsibilities that were central to the Executive Director position and indicated that he hoped the job would leave him sufficient time to pursue his own interests, including writing and making speeches about the work he had done in his prominent government position.

I was astonished that anyone would even consider the man's candidacy viable since he had made clear he wasn't really interested in doing most of the work the job entailed. But my fellow committee members were torn – not wanting to "give up the chance" to hire someone of the man's supposed stature. Mid-afternoon when the committee still had not come to a decision, the Chair said, "I'm going to go out on a limb with a somewhat daring proposal. Why don't we simply hire them both!" He proposed that the man, "who I'm just more comfortable with as the face of the Society," be hired to take on the leadership responsibilities of the position, and the current Executive Director be retained to carry out the day-to-day administrative responsibilities. "Of course, given his prominence," the Chair said referring to the man, "we would have to pay him more."

The white men on the committee indicated that they were intrigued by the idea and commended the Chair for his bold, original thinking. The lone white woman, who was in line to become the next President of the Society, said nothing. Emboldened by the realization that I had nothing left to lose, I took a deep breath, exhaled slowly, sat up in my armchair, and said, "This proposal is not only preposterous given the budgetary constraints the Society faces, but deeply offensive to me as a woman and a person of color." My comments were followed by stunned silence, then followed by the Chair's nervous call for a break during which the lone white woman told me, over the sound of flushing toilets in the ladies' room, how much she had appreciated my intervention. In the end, the woman of color was reappointed. It was the last meeting of the Society I would attend.

I could have flown from D.C. to New York but I chose to take the train because it was slower. I imagined the steady, rocking motion and the rumble of the wheels would make for a gentler and more grounded re-entry. I had traveled that train route countless times during the decade I spent in Washington. But as I sank into the upholstered seats of the business class compartment, I couldn't bring those years clearly into focus. I could see only what lay before me – the steel gray sky; the barren trees; the patches of brown earth beneath a blanket of blackened snow; the backs of tired buildings that lined the tracks – the warehouses, the abandoned factories, the sagging wooden homes whose small yards were miniature versions of the sprawling junkyards we occasionally rolled past. I drifted into sleep and woke up just as the train slipped into a tunnel blacker than the darkest of nights before gliding into the artificial light of Penn Station.

I thought I would be too impatient and distracted to negotiate New York City's subways, but as I worked my way through the station, pulling my suitcase across the smooth marble floor, hearing the familiar accent of veteran New Yorkers, I began to feel at ease. When I saw the sign pointing to the 8th Avenue subway line – the one that had carried me from Harlem to mid-town all those days of my young life – a rush of nostalgia propelled me toward the token booth and through its turnstile. I hadn't been on the subway in almost a quarter century but I knew exactly where to go and what to do.

When the subway train pulled into 135th Street it felt like 1965 again: I was fifteen years old and on my way home from school, full of energy and hope, with an oversized Afro, long skinny legs in a mini-skirt, and arms wrapped around a stack of algebra and Latin textbooks, topped off with a paperback *Lolita*.

The crisp, wintry air shocked my lungs into action. Heading up St. Nicholas Avenue, I passed the church where my mother had tried against my father's wishes to introduce us to religion; and then the rows of stately, remodeled brownstones whose empty stoops held the ghosts of rooming house tenants who'd shouted catcalls at my sister and me. I turned right on 139th Street, ran down to 8th Avenue, suitcase scraping an uneven pavement, and crossed against the light. When I came to our house, I looked around excitedly; secretly harboring a childish fantasy that people would come flooding out of the neighboring houses to greet the returning daughter. But the street was nearly deserted and all the doors and windows remained firmly shut. Pulling off my right glove, I gently placed a naked hand on the wrought iron railing and gazed up at the tarnished brass numbers, "262."

I was home.

Back Once More

꙰

STEVE WAS DRESSED in Wall Street business attire, the collar of his expensive cashmere coat pulled up around his neck. Jim the contractor was older, probably just into his sixth decade, and dressed more casually in understated LL Bean-style attire. He had a warm, appealing mustached face. The locksmith drove up just as we were finishing our introductions and set to work while the rest of us stood in front of the house, stomping our feet on the ground and breathing into our gloved hands, trying to dissipate both the chill and awkwardness.

Conversation faltered until the locksmith shouted, "Got it!" He turned and waited for one of us to come up the steps and push the door open. I urged Steve and Jim to go first, assuring them that I would be right behind.

"Are you ready?" Steve asked, looking back at me.

"I think so," I lied.

Steve leaned into the door but it resisted. Although my eyes could see it was because of layers of debris scattered around the tiled floor of the vestibule, my heart told me it was because the house was ashamed of how far it had fallen from its glory days.

I followed Steve and Jim in silence, encouraged to see that aside from the debris the vestibule appeared largely intact. Even the milk white globe that had lighted a thousand entrances by members of my family – some quite dramatic – remained in place, hanging securely from the high ceiling. The second elaborately carved wooden door separating the vestibule from the formal entryway was also intact, its etched glass window still covered from the inside by the sheer curtain my mother had installed so many years ago.

Without a single crack or blemish, a massive beveled glass mirror still graced the right wall to the entryway. I stared into it, standing in layers of dirt, fallen plaster and paint peelings, looking beyond myself.

There were picture hooks still in the walls to the right and left of the mirror with light-colored shadows where frames once rested. This had been a gallery of diplomas my father assembled: *Diplôme de Médecine* from

Université Libre de Bruxelles awarded to Ralph Thomas Mabry [father]; *Prix D'Excellence* awarded to Marguerrite Lillian Mabry [sister, 'Maggie'] by the Lycée Français de New York; AB, *Magna cum Laude* awarded to Linda Ann Mabry by Mount Holyoke College; *Diploma* awarded to William Gerald Mabry [younger brother, 'Jerry'] by the Choate-Rosemary Hall Academy; JD, with Honors awarded to Ralph Thomas Mabry, Jr. [older brother, known as Tommy by the family] by Cornell University – to name but a few. Dad would relish escorting visitors through this gallery, pointing out how much each one of those degrees had cost him.

I looked up expecting to see a stained glass light fixture that had hung in the entryway for more years than I'd been alive, illuminating all who passed through, but it was gone.

To the left of the entryway was the parlor – the place we had used as a formal living room. Drapes of thick gold fabric still hung in the windows, their linings frayed and stained. The custom sofa we had all been so proud of was still there, too, and I wondered why Mom hadn't taken it with her. Vina sat on that sofa the last time I saw her alive.

On the floor in front of the sofa lay a radiator that had warmed us through so many dark winters. It looked as if someone had torn it from the wall and thrown it across the room in a fit of madness. And then I saw it – the gaping hole where the exquisite fireplace mantle had been. I would soon discover that every single mantle, except the one in the second floor library, had been ripped out and carted off. The house had been scavenged.

As I worked my way toward the large foyer, I saw that thieves had carefully removed the majestic finials and spindles that defined our grand staircase. I knew I wasn't ready to climb those stairs so I retreated to the wall on the opposite side and reached out to touch the spot where our Baldwin upright piano once stood. Remembering how I had sat there hour after hour mastering the Bach *Inventions* and trying to master Beethoven's *Pathétique*, I heard a rush of notes and chords rising up the staircase toward the skylight on the top floor and imagined I felt the house quiver.

I moved from the foyer into the dining room and saw it buried under its own ceiling. There was plaster everywhere, in lumps and slabs and dirty powder. Someone – the City perhaps – had boarded up the tall windows at the rear of the room and I was glad for the darkness that kept me from seeing the full extent of the destruction.

There was nothing left of the kitchen. The floor had collapsed, leaving the remnants of the cabinets and appliances perched on top of a pile of rubble one story below.

Steve, Jim and I finished our tour of the house upstairs on the floor that housed the library and the master bedroom suite. The wallpaper Mom had hung in the master bathroom, with its oversized red and white pansy-like flowers linked by a web of slight green vines, clung stubbornly to the walls.

It was the only colorful thing left in the house. A tiled floor lay beneath layers of shattered glass from the collapsed light well that brought daylight into both the master bath and the children's bath one floor above. The large tub that Mom bathed in was still there, although the fixtures through which the hot water that soothed her weary body once flowed had been removed.

The library told the story of my parents' last days in the house. Pieces of torn window shades swayed gently in a breeze that blew through empty window frames. Plaster from the disintegrating ceiling covered the floor but the walls were mostly intact and still coated with yellow paint. Its fireplace mantel was also still in place, the only one the vandals hadn't taken. The room bore signs of a hurried exit. The desk from Goodwill sat proudly amidst the devastation. Pages from school notebooks were scattered around the floor. A roll of paper left over from the speed-reading machine lay on the floor. It seems in those final hours they just gave up trying to salvage what they had.

I have tried to understand why they didn't just sell Two-Sixty-Two, especially when the prices began escalating in the mid-1980s as Harlem experienced its second renaissance. It had long been clear that they would never return to Harlem. They had to know that a house cannot stand empty for twenty years and remain intact – they hadn't even boarded up the windows.

I think my parents were driven to hold on to Two-Sixty-Two by their past. Like many African-Americans of their generation, they believe strongly that real estate should never be sold. They grew up in the Deep South hearing stories from as far back as the days of emancipation of white people intimidating or tricking ignorant, illiterate blacks into selling them valuable properties for a song. They lamented the fact that my mother's family, who had been landowners, had not seen fit to pass those lands on to the next generation, but instead had sold them off and squandered the money. My parents said they wanted to be able to leave their children and grandchildren a tangible legacy. Maybe they also wanted to hold on to the dream – the dream that their purchase of Two-Sixty-Two was supposed to fulfill.

In many ways the library was the most important room in our house. It had been filled with textbooks of biology, mathematics, and history; flight instruction manuals; Reader's Digest compilations; a frayed copy of Jimmy Baldwin's *The Fire Next Time*; hardback comic books from our Belgian childhood; and a brightly illustrated collection of French children's songs. One of my favorite songs, *Marlbrough s'en va-t-en Guerre*[iv], although a dark tale of war and loss, was set to the cheerful, catchy tune of *For He's a Jolly Good Fellow*. I knew practically all of its twenty-one verses, and would sing my heart out, as if by sheer determination I could make joy out of sadness.

We finished our tour of the house and I stood in front of Two Sixty Two, warmly wrapped in my coat, long skirt and scarf. The massive, three-paneled door was behind me, recessed slightly in an arched enclosure decorated with brickwork that fanned out above a garland of limestone. At the top of the arch was an exuberant plume, the keystone, above it, a semi-circled window. The flagstone steps were worn where we and others had stepped and stood, pausing before entering or leaving. I had come back once more, this time seeking answers, hoping to make peace with the past, and finally on the path towards healing myself.

Taken on the day of her tour in 2001 – Linda outside Two-Sixty-Two, home again at last, and pleased at the prospect of fulfilling her parents' dream.

Conclusion

In late 2001, after returning from Harlem, Linda Mabry was diagnosed with pancreatic cancer. Her plans for Two-Sixty-Two were shelved as she entered treatment, and she never realized her dream of rescuing the house.

In 2005, Linda's father sold Two-Sixty-Two for $850,000. Two and a half years later in August 2007 a completely renovated house came on the market for $4.2 million.

Linda died April 4, 2007 of the pancreatic cancer she had fought for five years. A rift with her father that had developed during her illness was never resolved, and her brother Jerry was the only member of the family to attend her funeral.

In Linda's office after her death lay a blue folder. It contained handwritten notes, fragments of text, and multiple versions of draft chapters, evidence of a struggle to make narrative sense of her life.

For six months the binder remained untouched until Linda's husband, Dieter Folta, gathered several friends and colleagues around his dining-room table. Among them was Margarita Dalton, Linda's closest friend, to whom Linda had confided in her final days her wish to have her memoirs completed. With Dieter's encouragement, Colleen Crangle and David Gleeson reviewed the binder's contents, along with other material from her computer, and made a commitment to bring Linda's writing to publication.

Much of the work in the binder had begun to take shape in 2005 while Linda was attending Hedgebrook's writers-in-residence program – a rural retreat on Whidbey Island (off the Washington coast) where women writers gather from all over the world to work in community. While there she received the Adrienne Reiner Hochstadt Award, which honors one outstanding Hedgebrook writer-in-residence each year.

Bringing Linda's story to publication took much longer than anticipated. The first step was to draw up a timeline of her life and research the many topical and historical references in the writing. A narrative framework was chosen to contain its many diverse fragments, producing a story of her life in three parts. Colleen and David added accounts of their friendships with Linda, explaining why they took on this task, and why they care so much about Linda's story.

Three years after it began, in fall 2010, the work was finally completed.

COLLEEN CRANGLE

WE STOOD TOGETHER,
TWO AFRICAN AMERICANS

June 2009, Palo Alto, California

The voice on the other end of the line was strong and clear: "I'm Linda Mabry from the Stanford Law School. Can we meet? "

I was at home in my office, preparing a talk for the American Association of University Women (AAUW) in Palo Alto that night. I had been invited to tell my story, to explain what had led me a year earlier to file a discrimination and retaliation lawsuit against Stanford University. Two other women from the School of Medicine were to appear with me. I listened as Linda explained that something had gone very wrong at Stanford. She needed someone to talk to and a mutual friend in our Palo Alto neighborhood had given her my number. I said, come to the AAUW event, there will be other women from Stanford you can meet. She accepted without hesitation, asking only for the address and saying, I'll see you there. This interchange, with its directness and lack of guile, would turn out to characterize all our interactions; Linda wasted no time posturing or positioning herself.

A room full of men and women listened that night as I along with Dr. Jessica Agramonte and Dr. Julie Neidich, both from the Stanford School of Medicine, told of the gender bias we had encountered in bioinformatics, orthopedic surgery, and pediatrics at Stanford. We were not alone in our experiences of gender bias; we were simply the three women who at that time were prepared to speak out.

Afterwards, we stood together in the parking lot and listened as Linda, displaying an unexpected tentativeness, told her story. It was a little garbled, filled with auto-corrections such as 'maybe I got it wrong' and 'I'm not sure 'and a repeated cry, 'I don't know what to do.' What was clear was the

128

discomfort Linda felt with the very idea of discrimination, as if she could not bear to use the word in reference to her life. It was a dark night, with no moon, and in the unlit parking lot I never got a clear glimpse of Linda's face. But she was tall and had presence, even as she stood there in distress with her husband, Dieter, in his wheelchair at her side.

Linda soon threw her lot in with Jessica, Julie and me, adding her story to a comprehensive report we were preparing, charging wide-spread and systematic gender discrimination throughout the university in its hiring and promotion practices. The report contained 17 individual stories, the University's own reports on the status of women, and our compilation of most recent facts and figures. This 400-page document ultimately sparked a Department of Labor (DOL) investigation and class-action complaint. In addition to Linda, Jessica and Julie, our numbers included Dr. Karen Sawislak (a history professor whose successful tenure bid had been overturned by Condoleezza Rice, then Provost of the University), and Dr. Denise Johnson (the first African-American woman hired in the General Surgery Department). Together, we formed the nucleus of the 'Stanford Seven', a group that met regularly over the next several years at Joanie's Cafe, a popular eatery in Palo Alto that had tables spilling out onto the sidewalk. We would pull three or four tables together and, crammed up next to each other, share our lives. Unless Linda was away travelling with Dieter, she would be among us where she loved the camaraderie and gave empathetic support to the other women who joined us from time to time.

Our alliance was aimed at justice and girded by mutual trust. We shared stories of oversights and attacks on our credibility and competence that without examination would suggest we were each in our own way incomprehensibly deceived as to our capabilities. In each case, however, there was a history of accomplishment that gave the lie to the absurd idea that our experiences at Stanford were anything but the result of bias.

Living within a few blocks of each other on the leafy streets of Palo Alto, Linda and I grew close as I went through the grueling process of a federal lawsuit. She was the first person I called when, as happens in a drawn-out legal battle, there was a temporary setback or a toxic piece of correspondence from the university lawyers landed in my mailbox.

Linda and I collaborated on writing about gender and race equity. One day, appalled at the prospect of George W. Bush becoming president in 2000 and Condoleezza Rice possibly joining his Administration, we penned a letter to the Washington Post challenging Rice's integrity based on her record as Provost (the chief academic officer) at Stanford.[lvii] We sat at my dining room table as we worked on this letter, reveling in the pleasure of bringing our thoughts to life with words. We searched for a fresh phrase for the white men who at that time filled almost every position of power at Stanford. For 'white' we thought of 'pale people' and with our mood getting ever more frivolous we progressed to other designations until we blurted out almost in unison "pale people with penises in power! That's it." It was during these episodes of joint penmanship that I first noticed Linda's love of words, not surprising in an academic lawyer but striking nonetheless.

Even under the stress of walking out on Stanford, Linda stood tall and beautiful, with a posture that told of her love of dance. Yet she often observed that few people of color in entertainment or politics "looked like" her; rather they had the light skin and Caucasian features that she felt made them more acceptable to the public at large. What never ceased to amuse her was that with my blue eyes and pale sun-sensitive skin I was, as she put it, the "real African American."

Linda's play on words arose from my having been born and raised in Zimbabwe (then Rhodesia) and South Africa. It was truly as an "African American" that I responded to Stanford's actions against women and people of color, and Linda understood this immediately. She recognized the unique perspective on gender and race my background afforded me. [lviii] In South Africa, I was on the one hand the recipient of unwarranted privilege as a white and on the other unwarranted disadvantage as a woman. Atrocious conditions of gender inequity in South Africa caused a woman, for instance, to face the choice of becoming a legal minor when she married or forever being denied a share in the economic bounty of the marriage union, no property accrual being allowed to a woman who refused subordinate status. But while this distasteful option plagued white women up to the 1980s in South Africa, women of color were not even allowed a choice; the legal rights of adulthood were never even a possibility for them after marriage.

I first bumped up against the contradictions of being white and a woman in South Africa in my job at the University of South Africa as a recent graduate in the 1970s, Here I launched a campaign to extend to female faculty the same generous housing allowance only male faculty received, the assumption of the administration being that men had the responsibility to provide for their families and if a women wanted a house she had better find someone to marry. I aborted this campaign very soon, however, when I learned that no-one of color, male or female, was eligible for the housing allowance. I could not bring myself to expend all that energy on acquiring yet another white privilege, no matter how much I wanted that allowance.

There were very few black men working on the professional staff of the university, and not a single woman of color. Where possible I tried to get to know the few such men I encountered, believing that their intellectual journey had to be really interesting for it to have brought them into this bastion of white privilege where they had managed to secure a professional foothold.

No-one intrigued me more than the man I never got to know. He worked in the university library as a book handler, despite having a graduate degree. The word out on him was that he was denied a professional post commensurate with his education because, well, he was trouble. He was outspoken, the cardinal sin for a black man allowed to move in white circles.

I never looked at any person of color in the university the same way after being told about this man. Each person I saw, whether he was pushing a cart piled high with mail or she was straightening books in the library, prompted me to wonder about the potential that was being thwarted and hidden by apartheid's rule.

I thought about my own appointment and reassured myself that I deserved it and that I wasn't taking away a job that could or should have gone to a black man or woman. I was part of the country's first cohort of computer science students, with a *cum laude* degree and two teaching job offers before I'd even finished graduate school. Undeniable prejudice existed in employment, but other people were perpetrating these injustices, not me; I was just going about my business, wasn't I?

This cocoon of complacency was punctured by the big debate over the annual faculty dinner-dance. Apartheid laws prohibited multiracial gatherings at which alcohol was served. One can only imagine what unthinkable acts the authorities feared might take place with inhibitions lowered by alcohol. There was just one white faculty member in the entire university who objected to our compliance with this restriction. I heard him speak in the faculty senate meeting, passionately and with urgency, exhorting the decision makers to deliberately flout the law. The response from his colleagues was one of open derision, with snickers and sidelong glances. The older man sitting next to me in this my first faculty senate meeting whispered, "He's just overreacting because he lost his son in an accident. Never been the same since."

Although at 23 I was too young to grasp the loss of a child, as this man stood there alone near the bottom of the tiered auditorium, I didn't see someone made hysterical by misplaced grief. I saw someone whose pain had made him see suffering we were choosing to ignore. Paralyzed by the fear of making a fool of myself, I sat mute and stiff through the rest of the meeting. I never went to the dinner-dance but to this day I have also never stopped running the tape in my head that has me, or anyone, getting up and standing by that man's side in support. How different things might have been had we faced up to our complicity in the conditions of employment for men and women of color at the University of South Africa in 1975.

When Linda told me of the excuses her colleagues were making, attributing her behavior to the stress of seeking tenure and caring for a husband with multiple sclerosis, I again thought about that lone man standing in the auditorium at the University of South Africa, his colleagues trying to explain him away as a misguided emotion-driven fool. Any excuse being preferable to facing the reality of bias and our complicity in it.

* * *

When Linda was diagnosed with pancreatic cancer in 2001, after just a week or so of having strangely yellow eyes, she took on the disease as yet another challenge in a life full of conquests. She was, of course, terrified and she spoke with some bitterness about the illness that she believed was caused by the stress of Stanford. But it was as if, having been dealt this blow, she was going to be the very best cancer patient there was. With astonishing speed, she returned to regular exercise. Her home-cooked meals became plates of pure nutrition. I called on her at home one day as she was sitting down to lunch in her bright and airy kitchen, a blue and white room with a bay window on one side and a window overlooking her front garden on the other. On her plate were a piece of broiled salmon and a generous helping of lightly cooked spinach. I think I had grabbed a sandwich, with too much mayonnaise, for my lunch and I was in awe of her discipline.

Linda's cancer diagnosis did nothing to curb her healthy competitiveness. A late Joanie's breakfast with the Stanford Seven was scheduled for one day and, running late, I said I would see her there as a soon as I could drive over. She wanted to walk the two miles to the café. I expected her to be even later than me and was just telling the other women not to expect Linda for a while when in she came, a huge grin on her face. She had walked there in the time it took me to drive. Her triumph didn't stop there. She lifted the corner of her shirt and showed a fanny pack containing a battery-driven portable infusion pump that provided a continuous dose of chemotherapy drugs as she went about her daily post-operative life. She could go faster than me on foot *and* under treatment.

I used to visit a church in East Palo Alto whose ministers and congregation were primarily African American and I don't remember how it came about but one day Linda came with me. She had no declared interest in God or religion but was curious, I suspect, about the attraction the services held for me. Having grown up in Evangelical and Pentecostal churches I was completely at home with the upbeat music and hand-clapping sing-a-longs this congregation favored. I wondered how an intellectual atheist would respond. From the first resounding chord to the last drumbeat Linda was on her feet, swaying with unabashed enthusiasm and rhythm. I watched her with complete delight, for the first time, in some important way, seeing her completely at ease.

When Linda survived the surgery and follow-up treatment and was declared cancer free, we talked about this gift of time she had been given to finish her memoirs. As she said, "I have been fighting pancreatic cancer and so far I'm winning. Cancer gives you enormous clarity. I believe I'm still here because my work is not yet done."

She was fully aware of the appalling prognosis of pancreatic cancer, with a five-year survival rate of just four percent. Linda got her five years. In that time she continued her work at the library-based adult literacy center Project Read in East Palo Alto, the neighbor city to Palo Alto that in 1990 was fifty percent African American and in 1992 held the infamous title of murder capital of the country.

She also started work at an affordable housing non-profit in Palo Alto, cycling to work each day on her elegant English bicycle. One day I passed her in my car on a quiet street near the Palo Alto community center. I stopped to talk. The next time I saw her she was in hospice care, the cancer having returned with a swift deadliness. She died a few days later but before she did I sent her a note to reassure her that Dieter would be well cared for by her friends, knowing that her greatest worry was how he would fare without her. I had never made a promise to a dying friend before and I wondered how I would keep it. I wondered *if* I would keep it or if I would convince myself that my purpose was to comfort her as she lay dying and having accomplished that I had no real further obligation.

I told my daughter, Blair, about Linda's unfinished memoir. Blair was just three years old when I began my legal battle with Stanford and she was one of the reasons I fought so hard. I wanted to make sure that in 30 years time as she was launching her career no-one would dare suggest she serve as the Girl Friday to a male colleague who found her a threat. An exceptionally sharp young woman and even at thirteen a gifted writer, Blair said "You have to finish the memoir for her, mom."

I pointed out how little time I had outside of family and work but I loved the generosity of her thought and I told Dieter what she had said. His whole face lit up. We were having coffee at a table outside Peet's Coffee & Tea in the Town and Country center in Palo Alto, a series of low-slung Spanish-style buildings that house fancy clothing stores and the Hobees restaurant, a favorite eating place of Stanford students since 1974. Dieter's dog, Dakota, was lying on the paving next to him. With so many days of good weather in Palo Alto and so many outdoor tables, Dieter was able to take Dakota with him almost everywhere, his constant companionship a comfort.

To help Dieter put the question of Linda's memoir to rest, I agreed to go through Linda's home office with him. There we found a blue folder with a complete outline of her book. Many of the chapters were already written, others were in draft form, and her computer disk held all her files. My misgivings about my limited time started to dissolve. "I think we can do this," I said to Dieter with growing excitement, realizing that this act more than any other I could think of would fulfill my promise to Linda: Dieter would be given the gift of Linda's life story by her friends.

Within a month Dieter had gathered a group of Linda's friends and colleagues at his house to discuss compiling her memoirs. We met in his dining room. I sat next to someone from Linda's writing group in San Francisco. He had a quiet confidence about him and I liked him immediately. When he spoke I heard he was a Brit. Within a month, David Gleeson and I began to meet regularly to pull together Linda's story. We worked for close to two years, mostly at weekends, with David in the beginning carrying most of the load of collating all Linda's files.

Linda had left us much about her childhood and about her return as a 49-year-old to the Harlem house she lived in as a child. We were at first disappointed to find almost nothing about her college years, including the year she spent as a student in Africa. But as we knit together the strands of her writing, we realized she had left exactly the story she wanted to tell, one in which her Stanford experience while not defining her was the axis of balance in her life. It swung her around and took her all the way back to Harlem and then finally to a peace of sorts in quiet and pretty Palo Alto with her beloved husband.

DAVID GLEESON

HARLEM ON OUR MINDS

June 2009, San Francisco

'The coldest winter I ever spent was a summer in San Francisco.' Mark Twain

July in San Francisco can be colder than Mark Twain's headstone.

"This can't be worth catching hypothermia," I said to my friend Saeeda, teeth chattering, standing at the back of a line that snaked half-a-block down Market Street. It didn't seem worth waiting for an obscure reading series called Porchlight. I wanted to go home.

Leafing through the evening's playbill didn't exactly inspire us to stay, either: an obscure experimental poet, a radio host exhumed from the graveyard shift, a school bus driver with a cat named *Taco*, a "deceased sheep-lover," and a disoriented weight lifter – the stuff of which San Francisco is made, perhaps, but "It's freezing," I said. "Let's go."

If the speakers' bios weren't enough, then of all things off-putting, our program boasted a lawyer from Stanford with a new-agey sounding memoir, *Falling Up To Grace*. I pictured a squat, litigative, Deepak Chopra – leaking virtue and smugness from every pore.

By the time we'd elbowed our way into the hall it was packed. Saeeda led us to a patch of floor in the no-man's-land between footlights and a front-row of hecklers.

Bashing out chords as though with boxing gloves, a pianist limbered up for the first of many rounds. To be fair he was up against a swarthy looking opponent, missing many of its ivory teeth.

A referee explained the rules. The given theme was "Busted," and each speaker was allocated a strict number of minutes in which to extemporize. Anyone running overtime did so upon pain of piano – a punishment meted out with the utmost severity.

135

Variously posturing, pouting, vociferous or timorous, expounding in shades of good, bad and vanilla, the performers went about their routines, and always the piano came in brawling long before they were done.

I'd seen enough when the interval arrived. Again, I tried to persuade Saeeda to leave. No such luck. I was left as placeholder on the floor, while she went for a wander.

When she eventually returned with drinks, I said to Saeeda, "I thought we were leaving?"

"No," said Saeeda. "Because I just met my sister at the washbasins," she explained. "Well, she *should* be my sister. Anyway, she's up next – and we're staying."

With the grace and precision of a ballerina, Saeeda folded her legs, settled a yogic smile upon her face, and turned her attention to the stage.

Then a tall, black woman in her forties appeared in the spotlight, her face burnished golden brown. She paused and raised her chin. The sea of chatter parted in silence as if commanded by Moses himself. You could tell this woman didn't have a cat named *Taco*.

Her story led us gently through the back lanes of 1970s' New England with a young student at the wheel of an aging sky-blue Chevy II. Unsure and unused to country roads, she was driving from her own Mount Holyoke to the library at nearby Smith College in the process of researching a difficult paper.

Somewhere along the way the story turned into a cautionary tale, ostensibly about the hazards of smoking and driving, in truth about a black kid from Harlem astray in a bleach-white state. Her car had problems and needed water so she pulled up outside a small white clapboard house. Upon calling for help, no answer came. At the back of the house, she heard a small running stream and began scooping up water.

At some point during the storytelling I'd become so engaged I'd forgotten the discomfort of an un-swept wooden floor, and no longer cared if it was cold or even snowing inside. I was propelled through those lanes, until I could almost taste that water. Her story not only shone, it practically flickered with cinematic detail, as if projected onto our minds.

No sooner had the narrator brought one crisis under control, than another arrived: a man holding a shotgun inches from her face. We held our collective breath for her as she described a pair of weather-beaten white hands on the barrel. The man let fly epithets that might have hailed from sixties' Mississippi. Even in the context of segregation, persistent in the south until just a few years before, it was difficult to comprehend an attitude so stubbornly unreconstructed thriving among Massachusetts' elite.

When the story ended, no one stirred. Neither player nor piano dared leave their respective corners and risk breaking the dignity of the moment.

Then the clapping began, building to an intensity that left no room for doubt about the impression she'd made.

Several speakers later, all of whom must have rued following her performance, we filed out into the night.

Saeeda grabbed my arm and hurried us towards a minivan as its headlamps switched on. The woman from Harlem rolled down her window and introductions were made. "This is Linda," said Saeeda.

In person, Linda's smile and warmth seemed at odds with the woman who'd captivated an entire audience with her stage presence and command of storytelling.

It was past 11o'clock, and with the prospect of a 35-mile journey back to Palo Alto ahead, Linda couldn't chat for long. The drive was slow, she said, explaining her husband used a wheelchair, hence the need for a minivan.

We talked mainly about writing. Saeeda was halfway through a memoir concerning her childhood in Baltimore. I said I'd quit my job in pursuit of a book, and after two years of trying, I'd found myself most of the way broke and insane in the process. "Me too," Linda laughed.

Before leaving, Linda suggested the three of us meet again to compare notes.

Within a week, Linda and her husband, Dieter, had driven up from Palo Alto to my apartment in San Francisco. The evening got off to a bad start, my poor directions having misled them onto the Bay Bridge – a five-mile detour towards Oakland.

When the entry phone finally rang I went to meet them at the front door, offering apologies and help with the wheelchair. Too late, Dieter's turbo-motorized chair was already in the building and whizzing towards me. 'He's German,' Linda explained as Dieter rounded the corner ahead of us.

I took their coats and one of the other guests offered drinks. Perhaps being over-accommodating in my attempts to make up for bad directions, I micro-managed Dieter, anticipating his every move, offering food, drink, seating, lighting, heating and anything else that came to mind until he finally snapped at me, "I'm not a child!"

I tried to console myself with a British conceit that *the German sense of humor is no laughing matter* but Dieter quickly disproved this, showing himself to be as warm and good-natured as any of my fellow countrymen – if not more so.

We ate and talked, books and politics, books and writing, and more books. At some point, Linda pulled *King Leopold's Ghost* from my shelves and asked about its inscription to me from a friend's father. Then she told me of her childhood in Belgium.

Although the big hours became small hours and the small hours became morning, Linda and Dieter had under-stayed their welcome. There simply was never enough time. As they collected their things and prepared for the drive home, Linda relished the prospect of a reverse-commute with the sun coming up.

Before they left, the nucleus of a writing group had been formed, and we'd soon arranged a schedule of meetings, both in Palo Alto and different houses in the city.

In the months that followed, the strength of our friendship grew, and my admiration for Linda's writing with it.

* * *

Outside on the street that cold evening in San Francisco, Linda and I shared a fleeting moment to which it's hard to attach any importance, to all intents and purposes trivial. Me saying I quit my job to write – dismissive, self-deprecating, as though the career I'd had for twenty years meant nothing, as though the toll it had taken was of no importance, and as though the act of leaving had no more meaning than any of the tens of millions of decisions we take for granted in our lives, from brushing our teeth to crossing the street.

But I did care, and it made me want to know why Linda quit her job, too. I knew what having a 'good' job meant – status, self-esteem, prestige, wealth, (and solvency!) Beyond that, or perhaps underlying it, I could relate to an outsider's point of view. I'd left my own country because I'd never felt any sense of belonging there and when I tried to find it elsewhere it always felt like the seats were already taken.

But there was something else going on, something less easy to discern about what we held in common, beyond superficially both having quit our jobs to write. For very different reasons, we'd each set out to find something, not knowing at the outset what that might be, nor even what it could possibly look like.

It wasn't until the month after Linda died in April 2007 that a man named Obama (unnoticed by most of the country) declared an intention to seek the Democratic nomination. I don't know what Linda would have made of the events that followed in 2008. I do know that I felt compelled to trade in my green card for citizenship, sacrificing my ability to make quips about taxation without representation, but finally gaining the right to vote.

In September 2007, Dieter sent me Linda's 'blue binder,' asking for my opinion on what could be done with it. Reading through, I recognized a fair amount of the material, and wondered about many things.

What did I know of Harlem? The sum total of my experience was an attempt to cure a hangover back in the early 1990s. I'd walked from Wall

Street to 125th, looking for the Apollo, or Birdland [as I later discover, it never was in Harlem to start with, and in any case had long since ceased to exist], or that street where Thelonious Monk had stood alongside all the other jazz legends posing for a photograph that became *A Great Day in Harlem*. Crossing 96th, the environment felt anything but great. It was like crossing the 38th parallel, from one paradigm to another, from rules I understood to no rules at all – just as Linda had described it. I remembered looking around, and beginning to realize I didn't have the sort of drug habit that might warrant my being there. It was a neighborhood of derelict houses, boarded-up windows, kicked-in doors, and people who looked not at me but through me – their eyes haunted, and cheekbones hollowed beyond gothic. The only warmth I saw in twenty blocks was the flicker of a butane lighter beneath a crack pipe. By 125th and Lenox, I didn't know which way to turn, whether to risk walking back and be seen twice in areas I knew were scary, or keep going and find myself in worse.

With my entire working life spent in the music industry, I felt at least some part of my heart should have belonged to Harlem. From Coltrane to Coleman, from Monk to Miles, it's at least as significant, if not more so, as any stifling European court. Even if you don't like jazz, Harlem has inflected every note of 20th century music ever played. But all I felt that day was fear.

Re-reading Linda's account of her childhood intrigued me and renewed my interest in the place. It also caused me to reflect upon the challenges and threats she faced throughout her career, and what I'd been party to in my own.

Unlike Linda, I was never made to feel like 'the enemy,' although in a sense, I was. The music industry of the 1990s had it all: glamour, financial success, and more than its share of dissipation and bad behavior – for which it seemed we were richly rewarded. *I* was rewarded. No one around me registered a moment's guilt. Throughout decades of 'progress' – feminism, integration – the control room side of recording studios had remained an exclusively male preserve. Should this ever have occurred to its inhabitants, and it seldom did, then it was easily rationalized by noting that many if not most of the artists were women, and that the talent was black as often as white. Confirmation bias is a wonderful thing: so easy to find support for what you'd like to believe, so long as you don't look too hard.

Despite which, as far as getting Linda's manuscript published was concerned I wasn't motivated by guilt. I never thought of it as an amends that needed to be made.

On reflection, perhaps my biggest motivation was the fact that I loved Linda's story. The symmetry of an African-American family setting sail from Harlem – a town named by Stuyvesant who'd come from Haarlem – steering for what used to be the Netherlands. But the region they were returning to had since become Belgium, a country tainted with possibly the worst genocide in human history: at least fifteen *million* Africans died as a result of King Leopold's efforts to enrich himself. And now I was discovering how that country had provided Linda's father with a medical degree – all within a generation or so. There were plenty of people around young Linda in Brussels who'd been alive during those atrocities – and yet their fascination with colored skin was as if they'd never seen such a thing before – they seemed entirely ignorant of genocide, as was most of Europe. A thought that's still chilling to consider.

***

Few of us find the opportunity to put our lives on hold and take the time to examine and discover; to throw out the sacred cows to which we've been conditioned to attach so much importance; to be selfish, self-indulgent, self-absorbed and self-obsessed long enough to get to the root of some deeper truth about ourselves and those around us; without regard for the consequences, no matter how unpleasant we may find them to be.

While editing, I was afraid that one of the consequences for Linda might be her detractors seizing upon the emotional candor in her writing, adopting a kind of 'told-you-so' attitude, claiming, *She was unhappy from the outset, too unhappy to perform her job – and, look, her unhappiness had nothing to do with the Academy. Unlike us, she couldn't hack it, she was simply too weak.* Of course, rich white male academics who've thrived under the aegis of an entrenched elite, never having been discriminated against themselves, are bound to be impressed with the grasp they have on their own bootstraps, amazed at how high they can magically haul themselves. They would be. Leading such sheltered lives, they can almost be forgiven for mistaking unfair advantage as strength.

Too many times I've given an 'elevator pitch' for Linda's story, and at the mere mention of a black woman from Stanford and the word 'discrimination,' the listener will ask, by way of pointing out, 'Wasn't Condi a provost at Stanford?' As if the existence of one, conspicuously visible, black woman in a position of power were enough to quell the suggestion of legitimate grievance. The more I've learned in researching this memoir, the more I've come to realize, if anything, the opposite is true. That, in fact, entrenched powers can do more to reinforce their positions by careful choice of representative, preferably one with inherent contradictions – in much the same way they tried to use Linda. As highly visible as Condi's public profile may be, her agenda has always been anathema to the community she is taken to represent. For example, take her opposition to affirmative action, or her conservatism, cutting public spending, reallocation of resources to corporate interests, pursuit of wild neo-con foreign adventures at the expense of domestic policy… the list goes on.

In Linda's case, I think she found what she was looking for, and it wasn't in the shell of a house on Strivers' Row, or putting back together a family that was broken many generations ago on another continent – that would be more than all the King's men and all the King's horses could put together again.

I think what she found is captured in her words: the tragedy of racism is "that you doubt what you feel is a simple human yearning because you live in a culture that constantly denies your humanity."

***

On a chilly winter's evening in November 2008, which Mark Twain might've cursed, San Francisco braced itself for days of drawn out counts and recounts. Yet within hours a clear winner had emerged, and it was as though a closing chapter had been written for Linda's incomplete blue binder. As euphoric as that moment felt, it was bittersweet knowing how much more it would have meant to Linda. Solace lies in having had the gift of an opportunity to help finish the work she'd started – for which I thank both Linda and Dieter.

DIETER FOLTA

MOTHER NATURE THREW US TOGETHER, WE WERE ALWAYS TOGETHER

As told to Karen Sawislak

I first saw Linda in the fall of 1991. I was visiting a friend and colleague, Rick, at his house in Oakland on El Centro Avenue. El Centro was a hilly street, and I looked up and saw this woman on her balcony, working on the flowers that she had in planters.

She looked out at me and I looked up at her. I didn't know what hit me. I said immediately to Rick, "Why don't you tell her that I love her?"

For some time I had not been sure that I wanted to be in a relationship because I felt that my multiple sclerosis (MS) would mean that I would be a burden. But once I saw Linda, I didn't think about this anymore.

We didn't meet that day. Years later, I heard from a friend of Linda's that Linda had also noticed me. She told her friend that she had seen a cute guy from her balcony, who walked with a cane.

I went back to see Rick in Oakland in December. There she was again, standing on her balcony, working on her flowers. I asked Rick, "Did you tell her?" Rick and I walked over – he and Linda knew each other as neighbors.

I let Rick do the talking, and he proposed to Linda that we all get together soon, as neighbors and friends. I asked when. Linda suggested that we do it on that coming Friday. I couldn't make that date, because I was leaving for Europe and then for a holiday in Israel. So I told Linda that I would send her a postcard while I was gone. I wanted to be absolutely sure that I got her contact information!

We agreed that we would all have dinner on January 7 at Linda's house. Linda gave me her business card and we said goodbye for that day.

True to my word, I sent Linda a postcard from Israel. I also told my friend there that I had met someone.

When I came back to San Francisco, I had a message on my answering machine from Rick. While I was away, his relationship with his girlfriend had ended, and he had moved back to Colorado.

I knew I was going to keep my date with Linda and I called her right away. I told her there was good news and bad news. Linda asked to hear the bad news first. "Well," I said, "Rick and Elizabeth have broken up, so they are not coming." Then the good news: "I am coming."

When I went to her house on January 7, I had expected a few more people might be there. But I was the only guest. I was a little bit nervous because I would be alone with her, but I also felt relieved. She tried to make a vegetarian lasagna, which took her a long time. Later, I found out that she was nervous too.

We sat and ate and talked about everything and nothing.

Linda told me later, "As you were sitting in that chair I was falling in love with you."

At the end of the night when we were saying goodnight at the door I asked: "Can I hug you?" She said yes. We hugged and said goodbye.

I spent the next day with another friend. It was a Sunday, and we went to Golden Gate Park and to a movie. My friend asked if I wanted dinner, and suggested sushi. I knew already that Linda that liked sushi and I very much wanted to see her again, so I called her to ask if she would join us for dinner. But she was not at home so I left a message on her answering machine.

I was very happy when Linda called me later that evening when I was back at home. She had missed my call because she had been working. We talked for a while, and I was trying hard to figure out a way to see her again very soon. At one point Linda said she was going down to Stanford for an interview the next day. I told her that I was working nearby, and asked her stop by when she was heading back to Oakland. When we said goodbye, I hoped I had convinced her to come to see me, but I wasn't sure.

She did stop to see me after her day at Stanford. We sat in my office in Belmont and talked for a long time. We drove together back to Palo Alto and had dinner. We talked more about our lives, about what it was like to be single and to have a career.

At the end of the night, Linda asked to come back to my apartment. So we did. This time, Linda didn't leave for three days. And that was the beginning and end of it – we were together.

We always spent a lot of time with each other. In the spring, Linda took a break from her work as a lawyer, before starting a semester of teaching at Stanford on a trial basis.

Since she had the time, we took our first trip together. Linda and I drove to Colorado, to attend a meeting for people with MS and their partners. I was having some struggles about coming to terms with my disease and Linda came with me. On our way back, driving through

Arizona, we were in a terrible car accident, and a man was killed. This brought us together even closer. We didn't want to be alone after that.

We found out soon that we balanced each other and complemented each other very well. Linda was a morning person and I am an evening person. After the accident, I would cry in the morning and she would cry in the evening. When one of us was weak, the other was strong. This was true for everything that life threw at us.

That same year we took a trip at Christmastime back to Europe. We were surprise guests at the wedding of my niece. It was a great event -- the whole family finally could meet.

My family loved Linda – her unbelievable smile and charm, her interest in others, and her huge heart. They all saw that immediately.

Linda wanted to know the details of my life. She wanted to see where I grew up and to understand my family. In April of 1993 we went back to my hometown and we also went to Brussels, where Linda had lived as a girl.

Linda got her job at Stanford and we decided to buy a house together in Palo Alto. Linda took the lead in hunting for the house, and had decided that it needed to be one story, because of my MS. I provided the down payment and Linda took care of the monthly payment – we always tried to make arrangements like this, that worked for both of us. We married here in our garden in October of 1993.

We were very similar but very different. For us, the other person accepted the other person – but maybe we tried to change the other a little bit too.

Sometimes when I look back and think about what attracted us to each other, I think about the fact that Linda spent so much of her childhood in Europe. Then she lived in New York. I too always was living abroad. When you are living outside of your own country, you are always a little bit of a maverick or outsider. You do not quite fit in, 100%. You are always asking, where are your roots?

From the moment I saw her, it was clear to me that we would be together. We found our home with each other.

Linda and Dieter, Death Valley.

In Celebration
of an Extraordinary Life

Linda A. Mabry

April 30, 1952 - April 4, 2007

A service will be held
Tuesday, May 22, 2007
at 4:30 p.m.
First Presbyterian Church
1140 Cowper Street & Lincoln
Palo Alto

A reception will follow honoring Linda's
fondness for good food and conversation.

community-based non-profit organizations including Project Read an adult literacy project in East Palo Alto and the Oakland-based Savage Jazz Dance Company, where she was a board member. Linda continued working until March 2007, holding the position of Below Market Rate Housing Administrator at the Palo Alto Housing Corporation where she began in 2003.
Linda traveled extensively throughout Europe, Africa, and Latin America. Her energy and abiding curiosity of life and people made friends wherever she went, and her infectious smile and laugh will be missed by friends, clients, colleagues and family. She will live long in our hearts.

In addition to her husband, Dieter Folta, and stepson, Olaf Folta, Linda is survived by her parents, Ralph and Gwendolyn Mabry, brothers Ralph Jr. and William, sister Marguerite and three nephews and three nieces.

In memory of Linda, her husband Dieter Folta has established the Linda A. Mabry Foundation. The foundation's goal is to fund projects for African-American children and youth in East Palo Alto. Contributions can be made payable to the Linda A. Mabry Fund c/o Community Development Institute, Post Office Box 50099, East Palo Alto, CA 94303.

Linda A. Mabry
April 30, 1952 – April 4, 2007

Linda A. Mabry, a writer, teacher, lawyer, community activist and more importantly beloved wife, friend and, aunt, passed away peacefully in Palo Alto, California. Linda was 54 years old and continued to live an active life having survived pancreatic cancer for more than five years. She was a courageous and inspiring person to many people in her life. To have known her was an honor.

Linda devoted her life to community involvement in public and private sectors and pursued what was most meaningful in her life – writing and teaching others about living life with purpose, and advocating for justice and equality in racial issues and political causes. Linda nurtured her friendships and enjoyed dancing, music, art, travel and being in nature. Linda enjoyed life with her husband of 16 years Dieter Folta, and their dogs Kai and Dakota.

Linda's death is a loss to her family, friends, community and society as she was a 'truth seeker' in its truest meaning. Linda wrote numerous articles that were published in trade journals, newspapers and magazine, on justice and equality related to the dignity of the human person and her African-American heritage. Linda's most recent project was writing her unfinished memoir entitled, *Falling Up to Grace*. In 2005 she was in residence at Hedgebrook, a retreat for women writers on Whidbey Island in Washington State, where she was awarded the Hochstadt prize for her work-in-progress. Linda was honored to receive this award. Her writing will continue to live on – in and through so many of her fans and loved ones.

Linda was born in New York and raised in Brussels, Belgium and Harlem. Linda excelled in anything she devoted her attention to, including academic pursuits at Mount Holyoke College and Johns Hopkins University School of Advanced International Studies and graduating with a law degree from Georgetown University in International Law. Linda was an attorney-Advisor in the Office of Legal Advisor of the U.S. Department of State from 1978-1981. She then practiced law between the years of 1981 through 1986 at Hogan & Hartson and Miller & Chevalier in Washington, D.C. Linda arrived in the Bay Area in 1986 and joined the San Francisco law firm of Howard, Rice, Nemerovski, Canady, Robertson & Falk in 1987 and later became a partner in their Corporate Department. In 1993, she became Associate Professor at Stanford Law School where she remained for five years teaching International Business.

Linda's long illustrious accomplishments and credentials pale compared to her unmoving commitment as an active volunteer in

Thoughts on Life

Be fully present

Tell your truth

The story is never finished

Be irreverent

Laugh at life

Make a difference in
someone's life every day

Eat what you enjoy

Question authority

Live each moment to its fullest

Things I Have Loved Doing
By Linda Mabry

Dancing
- The feeling of being one with the music and the other dancers when distinct steps and moves became a dance.
- Being able to express and convey deeply felt emotions through physical movement.

Speech Writing and Public Speaking
- Crafting words into language that conveyed deeply felt emotions and strongly held beliefs about important personal and social issues.

Cooking and Entertaining at Home
- The act of making food: conceiving the meal – reading through recipe books and conceiving the meal, imagining the taste and texture and appearance of the food; handling the raw ingredients – chopping, mixing, etc.
- Watching the evening come together: the guest begins to relax and enjoy each others company; the conversation begins to flow.

Student Counseling
- Connecting with young people full of energy and optimism and idealism. Guiding them around or at least warning them of the "pitfalls."

Antique Hunting
- Searching for hidden treasures. Touching, feeling, smelling objects of times past, imagining the past lives evoked by those objects.

Traveling Abroad
- Exploring foreign lives. Exploring beautiful landscapes and architecture. Mastering foreign cultures and languages.

PRESS ANNOUNCEMENTS

San Jose Post Record[3]
September 2, 1993

At Stanford, practitioner makes perfect
International trade and business lawyer Linda Mabry is the newest faculty member at Stanford Law. Mabry takes her practical experience in the field straight into the classroom.
By Jane Baile
POST-RECORD STAFF WRITER

Linda Mabry, Stanford University law school's newest professor, wants to instill in her students a sense of importance and complexity for international trade and business law.

Mabry, 41, the second African American hired by the school in its 77-year history, recently left the San Francisco firm of Howard, Rice, Nemerovski, Canady, Robertson, Falk & Rabkin where she had become partner in 1991.

Mabry first came to the law school in the fall of 1992 as a visiting lecturer. She said that she was considering a career in academia, and had contacted Professor Bill Hutton, a former colleague of hers at Howard, Rice who now teaches tax law at the Hastings College of Law in San Francisco.

When Hutton and Mabry met in the Spring of 1992, he encouraged her to seek an academic career and helped her contact the associate dean at the Stanford Law School. It turns out that faculty recruiters had been looking for someone with international experience, Mabry said.

She impressed faculty members and administrators with her "wealth of experience and enthusiasm" in the area of international business law, said Paul Brest, law school dean.

"I think she will serve as a model of a professor who brings a great deal of practical experience and combines it with a serious dedication to scholarship," he added. "We are very excited and pleased to have her as a colleague."

Her first class this fall will be a broad survey course that will examine a range of international transactions, from export sales to setting up foreign subsidiaries. Mabry wants her students to understand that when representing clients in other countries, attorneys must be familiar with a variety of additional issues that do not exist in domestic transactions relating to foreign exchange rates, treaties, different cultures and "a sense of the interplay between national, international and regional legal regimes."

Her proposed scholarship agenda at Stanford includes writing about trade and investment laws and institutions particularly on economic development.

"The challenge of this next century will be to reduce or eliminate some of the disparities in income and standards of living between the northern and southern hemisphere," she said. "The challenge will be to resolve these issues that arise in the context of north-south relations."

Mabry said she would also like to continue her work on national security issues on trade and investment. Whereas many of the current export controls were established in the 1940s to hinder the Soviet Union from acquiring such technology, Mabry said that the current global situation calls for a set of regulations that recognizes the need for countries to acquire certain technologies for development purposes while guarding against the proliferation of defense-related systems such as nuclear weapons.

Mabry's interest in international issues began at an early age. When she was four, in 1956, her family left their native New York City and moved to Brussels so that her father could attend medical school there. Mabry said that educational opportunities were limited for many African Americans in the United States at the time, and her father felt that he could receive a better medical education at a European university.

Her family returned to New York City in 1962, where her father established a general medical practice on 116th Street in Harlem.

She and her older brother were enrolled at the Walden School, an institution premised on the ideals of Henry David Thoreau, while her younger brother and sister attended the Lycée Français in order to hone their French skills.

Growing up in Harlem sparked Mabry's academic and professional ambitions, as she said she saw what could happen to people who were unable to move beyond the physical and mental ghetto environment.

After high school she attended Mount Holyoke College, an all-women school in South Hadley, Massachusetts. Mabry said she was attracted to the college for its emphasis on female students and its relatively rural New England setting.

"You come out of an institution like that with a stronger sense of who you are and a stronger sense of what you can do," she said. "And the aesthetics of my environment have always been very important to me."

In 1971, during her junior year in college, Mabry traveled to east Africa, where she attended Makerere University in the capital of Uganda.

"I went in part out of what was then a newly emerging interest among African Americans to find out where they were from," she added.

At that time, it was one of the most prestigious universities in Africa. Mabry said she also looked forward to studying African politics in an African context.

The experience taught her that even though she was of African descent, she was not African. Mabry arrived at Makerere with an Afro hairstyle, something that she tried to explain to her classmates was a sign of African heritage among those living in the United States. Yet, Mabry said that many of her fellow students in Uganda found this hairstyle a strange symbol of African heritage since they wore their hair short due to the region's warm temperatures.

She said she also found many of the students cliquish along their tribal, regional or national lines, and the precarious security situation under then-dictator Idi Amin made her appreciate the relative physical security she said she felt in the United States.

After graduating magna cum laude with a degree in political science in 1973, Mabry decided to earn a masters degree at the School of Advanced International Studies at Johns Hopkins University in Washington, D.C. Mabry said she found herself interested in economic and legal issues in the context of international relations and decided to attend law school.

She entered the Georgetown University Law Center in 1975 and focused much of her time on international law.

She served as president of the association of Student International Law Societies, president of James Brown Scott Society of International Law, editor of the Law and Policy in International Business publication and executive editor of the Association of Student International Law Societies International Law Journal.

During law school Mabry worked part time as a law clerk in the international maritime and aviation division of the U.S. Department of Transportation and the law firm of Gindburg, Feldman & Bress in its energy law department. She also served as a French-English interpreter for the U.S. Department of State.

Mabry's first job out of law school in 1978 was as an attorney-adviser in the Office of the Legal Adviser at the State Department, where she worked on cases involving international transportation, international judicial assistance, foreign bribery, debt rescheduling, international commodity agreements, economic development and investment assistance programs and treaty law. Two years later she went to work for the U.S. Department of Commerce as a special assistant to Homer Moyer, the organization's general counsel.

Over the next few years the two collaborated on a long article on exports controls, which was published in a revised form in 1985 as a book entitled Export Controls as Instruments of Foreign Policy.

Mabry said she chose to work in the public sector after law school since it would allow her to understand how governmental agencies formulate policy decisions.

Her decision was also made easier at the time since the salary discrepancy between the private and public sector was significantly less than it is now. Mabry said that while she was offered $118,000 a year by the State Department, her fellow law school students who decided to work for law firms made an average of $25,000 their first year.

But after three years as a government attorney Mabry moved to the private sector at the suggestion of one attorney whom she met while at Georgetown, who advised her that the highest ranking government jobs went to those who had been successful in the private sector.

Mabry's first job as a private attorney was at the Washington, D.C., firm of Hogan & Hartson, where she specialized in corporate and commercial law.

Half-jokingly, she described her private sector business lawyer job as turning a handshake into 20,000 pages of documents. Several feet of dark blue binders holding such transactional records now line her Stanford University office.

After one year at that firm, Mabry left to join Moyer, her former Department of Commerce boss, at the Washington, D.C., firm of Miller & Chevalier. She would remain there for four years, practicing international trade law.

Mabry said she began to become disenchanted with certain aspects of the Washington legal practice and social scene. She said that many legal and legislative professionals did not always understand what it meant to run a company and she realized that many of her friends had left the Washington, D.C., area.

In 1985 Mabry said she began to consider other careers, such as banking or in-house counsel positions.

"I wanted to see more of the transactional side" of corporate law, she said, which meant a move to Wall Street or a particular company's headquarters.

One year from partnership at Miller & Chevalier, Mabry left the firm in 1986 and moved to Oakland, California to the firm of Helm & Purcell, which evolved from the general counsel's office at the Computerland Corporation. The venture gradually moved back to in-house and Mabry left the firm in the summer of 1987 to join Howard, Rice, Nemerovski, Canady, Robertson, Falk & Rabkin.

Three years later she made a partner, and soon thereafter started thinking seriously about leaving the practice of law for a teaching career.

Since returning to academia, she said she has come to realize that "My happiest times were as a student."

***

Daily Journal[4]
Thursday February 11, 1999

Stanford Students Protest Professor's Departure - Officials Decline to Comment on the Resignation of Lone Black Woman
By Michael Moline

Stanford University Law School Dean Paul Brest met with several hundred students for two hours Wednesday amid mounting concerns over the recent abrupt resignation of the only black woman faculty member on tenure track at the law school.

Linda Mabry left Stanford at semester's end in December, having tendered her resignation "around that time," Brest said in an interview following his session with the students.

But he declined further comment on her departure, both in his meeting with the students and in the interview, saying employee records are confidential.

"I'm certainly not going to comment on why she left," Brest said.

Mabry could not be reached for comment. According to Brest, the courses she had been scheduled to teach in international trade law and international business transactions during the current semester have been canceled.

Of the 40 full-time law school faculty at Stanford, there are nine white women and five male members of minority groups, including four blacks and one Hispanic, Brest said. Mabry had been the only black woman up for tenure at the time of her resignation.

The development followed reports that the U.S. Department of Labor has opened an investigation into affirmative action violations at Stanford, although Brest said the law school compared favourably to the nation's other top-ranked schools on diversity.

The dean said Wednesday's meeting was not directly related to Mabry's departure, but rather was called to discuss "concerns about faculty diversity."

"It's a perennial issue," he said.

But Dominique Day, a third-year law student and member of the Black Law Students Association, said unhappiness over Mabry's departure swelled

---

attendance at the session. Students filled the auditorium's 200 seats and crowded along the walls, she said.

Day is helping draft a list of demands related to minority faculty hiring and retention, agreeing with Brest that the issue won't die.

Indeed, she added, student manifestos about the topic have been gathering dust at Stanford since the 1970s.

"It's the same conversation," she said. "Sometimes it's the same conversation with the same dean. It's the same list of demands. It's the same remedies [proferred]."

Day said Mabry's departure should be viewed in the context of "the history of a long-term apparent hostility towards faculty of color, particularly women faculty, and to separate the issue of Linda Mabry from the bigger issue that allows things like this to keep happening."

***

Daily Journal[5]
Friday February 12, 1999

Black Stanford Professor Tells Why She Resigned – Linda Mabry Says She Quit Because of a Pattern of Bias: 'I Was Made to Feel Invisible'
By Michael Moline

Her father tried to warn Linda Mabry not to accept a job offer from Stanford Law School and to steer her instead to the historically black Howard University. But somehow his message didn't get through.

"I was really angry at that [suggestion], because I thought that getting to Stanford was such an achievement," Mabry recalled Thursday. "And today I have to admit he was probably right."

Mabry had been the only black woman on tenure at Stanford Law, but in December she abruptly resigned. In an interview Thursday, she explained that her walkout was forced by the professional humiliation she felt when the law school launched a new program in her field of expertise without consulting her.

"That act to me was a clear indication that I would be subject to the same kind of egregious treatment that had been a pattern with respect to people of color at the law school," Mabry said.

"I resigned because I came to the conclusion that Stanford Law School is not a hospitable place for women and people of color and in particular women of color."

Mabry is among more than a dozen female professors and researchers whose discrimination complaints against Stanford University are being investigated by the U.S. Department of Labor. Stanford must meet federal guidelines for hiring and promoting women and minorities or risk losing about $500 million annually in federal grants and contracts.

Dean Paul Brest has declined to comment on the particulars of the Mabry case, while defending Stanford Law's record on diversity. Meanwhile, other university officials, including Provost Condoleezza Rice, are on record opposing affirmative action in granting faculty tenure.

Of the 40 full-time faculty at Stanford Law, there are nine white women and five male members of minority groups, including four blacks and one Hispanic, according to Brest. Mabry had been the only black woman up for

---

tenure at the time of her resignation.

Mabry joined the law school in 1993. At that time, Brest praised her in a statement released by the university.

"She will play a key role in preparing our students for a future in which business, trade and information are increasingly global," Brest's statement promised.

Instead, Mabry said, she was used to help raise funds for a new program in trans-national business law but frozen out of the planning for the project. She said she had 15 years' experience in the field before joining Stanford, including service with the Carter administration. She left a partnership position with San Francisco's Howard Rice Nemerovski Canady Robertson & Falk to join Stanford.

"I am the principal international law faculty person at the law school," she said. "I am the only one who writes specifically in that area, and I'm the only one who has significant practice experience in that area."

Yet, Mabry described being blind-sided by the creation of the trans-national business project.

"I found out about a program established in my curriculum by seeing a flier posted on a student bulletin board. I mean, brochures had been printed," she said.

"It was personally devastating to find that my colleagues not only thought so little of me, but [that they] didn't even think about me. I wasn't even a blip on the radar screen," she said. "It's worse than being mistreated. It's being completely invisible."

While federal officials investigate the broader situation at Stanford, Mabry is pursuing an individual discrimination complaint that is now in mediation. But she can't imagine ever going back to work at Stanford.

"I can't walk into the law school building without suffocating. My colleagues won't look me in the eye," she said. With a few exceptions among the faculty, "no one has stood up for me, and that hurts more than anything."

Mabry said the incident should be viewed in a broader context of often subtle preferential treatment for whites, and particularly white men, at the nation's legal institutions, including law schools. For example, she said, if white male students can't relate to minority lectures, the lecturer might get blamed for being a poor teacher, while ineffective white male teachers are coddled as eccentrics.

"The reason it's so difficult for minorities, particularly African-Americans, in the academy is that one of the most pervasive stereotypes about us is that we are intellectually inferior. That is what is at the heart of the difficulties we're having," Mabry said.

"You have to be perfect on everything, and even that's not good enough. If I can't be there, I don't know who can."

Mabry said she hasn't worked since resigning and isn't sure what her next professional move would be. She is considering moving to Europe, where she was raised while her father attended medical school.

She noted that in the United States, the attrition rate for black women in law firms is 87 percent.

"The bar keeps getting raised. They can't argue that there aren't any qualified women or minority lawyers – we've been coming out of the best law schools in the country for 20 years. But it's about the subtle ways in which you're excluded. The things to which you're not invited, the conferences and conversations that you're not a party to, the failure to introduce you to clients."

"I'm tired," she said. "I'm not going to put myself through this again. If I go to practice, I'll set up my own firm, I'll work for a firm where there are only women and minorities, because I'm tired of having people question my humanity."

She added: "If I were to teach again, Howard looks really good.

***

The Stanford Daily Staff[6]
Friday February 12, 1999

Mabry speaks out – Fmr. law prof. alleges racism
By Ritu Bhatnagar

Former Law School Prof. Linda Mabry spoke out yesterday about "the law school's racially hostile environment" for the first time since her abrupt resignation in December.

"I left Stanford law school because it is an institution that engages in a pattern of practicing intense bias, which devalues, discourages and marginalizes people of color," Mabry said.

Mabry is one of the professors who decided to file complaints with the Labor Department concerning the University's tenure practices.

"These institutions have never been held accountable for their actions to the students and the public," Mabry said. "They've hidden behind this veil of truth and scholarship, when their real actions are certainly not reflective of 'justice.' I issued these complaints with the hope that someone would hold them accountable, that the Labor Department will deem them responsible."

Law School Dean Paul Brest held a town hall meeting on Wednesday, where he discussed diversity issues with faculty and students. While Mabry's resignation was never directly mentioned, Brest addressed student concerns over minority faculty departures in the past few years.

"Minority faculty who have left over the years often had other offers or personal issues causing them to leave," Brest said.

Mabry, however, took a different stance. "[Brest] is certainly entitled to his own view, but when people of color are leaving, not because of money or because they are lured away by Harvard, there is a serious, racial problem," she said. "There is a 100 percent attrition rate for women of color, and only two women of color have been on the tenure track in the Law School's 106-year history. The Law School dehumanizes minorities, and yes, [Brest] is right, I do take it personally – very, very personally."

At the town hall meeting, Brest cited statistics that indicate Stanford is the most racially diverse law school in the nation. Minorities make up 12.5 percent of Law School faculty.

"We are a small law school of about 40 faculty members," said Xavier Gutierrez, a second-year law student. "We do have one tenured Latino professor, two African-American tenured professors and two African-

---

[6] Reprinted with permission of *The Stanford Daily*.

American junior faculty members. This is sizable for a small law school, but I obviously think many more need to be brought in to equalize."

Mabry said she was skeptical of statistics that measure what she calls a "revolving door."

"Minority faculty, both tenured and tenure-track, come and go, and the University may replace them with other minorities, but that means the faculty isn't a consistent body," she said. "When professors must continually leave, this harms the institution and its students."

Mabry describes her six years at the Law School as if "you're being asked to run a race in lead boots, while white men sail along on winged feet."

Mabry recalled a particular incident in October that she said largely contributed to her decision to leave the Law School.

"I found out, by seeing a flier on a student bulletin board, that the Law School was establishing a transnational business program," she said. "I am the only faculty member that teaches transnational business law. I was not consulted about the formation of this program, which I found highly disrespectful."

"Basically, they used me in the incipient stages of the program to raise money from an outside source. I went to dinners and lunches with potential donors and rolled out for the dog and pony as the token minority. Then, after they got the money, they handed the reins to someone else, who - while he is talented – is a half-time professor and is not even in transnational business. It's as if I don't count at all."

According to Mabry, the program is being headed by Law Prof. Thomas Heller, whose specialty is international law and economy.

Mabry came to Stanford in 1993 after practicing law at a variety of prominent firms; she said she was "publicly acknowledged by the Clinton administration in 1992 and 1996" for her contributory work.

"I'm not a megalomaniac who wants to be in charge of everything," she said. "I just ask that I be told when a program in my field of expertise, of which I am the only faculty member in the school, is instigated."

While this incident was key in her decision to leave, Mabry felt the general environment at the Law School was also a strong factor.

"When students cannot accept the expertise of a woman of color and will do so willingly for a white man, who may be less of an expert, this is deeply painful," she said. "And then there are colleagues who will subtly dismiss your work as 'garbage,' though they have little knowledge in the field but just have an objection to the color of your skin."

While Marcus Cole, an African-American tenure-track law school professor, declined comment on the issue, another one of Mabry's colleagues, Law Prof. William Gould, mostly concurred with her views. "I thought that I had encountered in the past, situations similar to what

[Mabry] encountered," he said. "I think that the fundamental problem, which Dean Brest has tried to address, is that minorities are in many or most instances invisible people."

According to Gould, Brest has attempted to address issues of diversity more so than his predecessors.

"[Brest], to his credit, has been quite focused and interested in diversity issues," Gould said. "When [the Mabry situation] emerged, [Brest] attempted to engage many of us, minority and non-minority in discussion."

In relation to Mabry's views, Brest maintained that he was "very sorry that [Mabry] feels this way."

"I've looked into this matter very seriously," Brest said. "I knew what her concerns were when she left, and I met with many faculty members to discuss this. The conclusion that I reached was that she was not treated in a manner different from other faculty members."

Mabry, however, disagreed with Brest's assessment. "I have put my professional life on the line in doing this, so obviously I must have very disturbing and important reasons. When you see people who look like you being disrespected, when you see this pattern of disrespect being forced on you, it's basically like saying, 'Linda Mabry, you don't count.' "

Brest has organized meetings to be held in the coming weeks with the Faculty Appointments Committee and the Student Liaisons Committee to discuss diversity issues that Mabry's case has catalyzed.

"I think it's very important that we get someone from outside the Law School to determine how and if we have created a hostile environment and how to fix that," said Beth Ybarra, a third-year law student.

Mabry has not made her plans for the future. "I have to work; it is my livelihood," she said. "But the way I'm feeling right now, I can't see myself going back to teaching for a while."

***

San Francisco Chronicle[7]
Monday February 15, 1999

Shadow on Diversity At Stanford / Spate of Faculty Departures Dismays Black Law Students
By Bill Workman
Chronicle Staff Writer

STANFORD -- The embittered resignation of a popular black professor has raised new questions about Stanford Law School's ability to retain minority and female faculty, even as the federal government looks into allegations that the university has broken affirmative action laws.

Professor Linda Mabry, who taught international business law for six years, left abruptly in late December. Her resignation was prompted by what she described as the law school's "inhospitable environment" for minorities.

The law school "engages in a pattern of practicing bias that demeans, devalues, marginalizes and excludes people of color," she said.

Despite an extensive background in international business law in both government and private practice, Mabry said she was overlooked as a potential choice to head up the school's new Transnational Business Law program.

Mabry said that when the school first began seeking grant money for the program two years ago, she had been "rolled out for the dog-and-pony show as the token minority." She felt betrayed when she was not notified that the program was established and that Associate Dean Thomas Heller had been put in charge.

Mabry, 47, is one of 15 female professors and researchers at Stanford who have complained to the U.S. Labor Department that the university violates federal anti-discrimination law in the hiring and promotion of women.

The agency's Office of Federal Contract Compliance Programs is looking into the allegations. Stanford has more than $500 million in federal contracts that could be in jeopardy if violations are proved.

Law School Dean Paul Brest labeled Mabry's allegations as "entirely inaccurate."

---

[7] Republished with permission of the Hearst Corporation, from "Shadow on Diversity At Stanford: Spate of faculty departures dismays black law students" by Bill Workman in the San Francisco *Chronicle*, Monday February 15, 1999; permission conveyed through Copyright Clearance Center, Inc.

While declining to address her complaint that she had been slighted by the school, he took pains to point out that as associate dean, Heller is in charge of all international programs and that the new one had evolved under his direction since it was first proposed.

Brest conceded that his law school has had significant faculty turnover, "white, black and Latino." He attributed it largely to offers from other schools, or for reasons that had nothing to do with disenchantment with Stanford.

He maintained that Stanford is the "most racially diverse" of the nation's elite law schools, with five minority professors on its 40-member faculty who have either permanent status or are on a tenure track. By comparison, he said, "Yale has none." In addition, Brest said Stanford Law has nine female faculty members.

On the undergraduate level, a nationwide survey of black college educators published last month ranked Stanford almost as highly as well-regarded historically black universities for providing an environment in which African American students can flourish.

Stanford is ranked 10th, even though its African American population, at 8 percent of the student body, is vastly smaller than such well-known black institutions of higher education as Spelman, Morehouse, Howard and Tuskegee, which all scored higher than Stanford. The top nine were all historically black institutions, and Stanford's Ivy League competitors for the best and brightest students finished much further down in the survey's top-50 list.

At the law school, Mabry's sudden departure ignited a fresh round of criticism from minority and other law students over what Mabry called the "revolving door" turnover in minority faculty.

"Almost every year, we're seeing people of color leave the law school," Dominique Day, a third-year African American law student, told a "town hall" meeting Brest held with students last week to discuss the issue.

Day, a member of a student committee that meets regularly with the faculty on appointments, noted that for the past decade the law school has expressed a commitment to diversity, "but it seems only to lead to the exodus of (minority) faculty."

Even before Mabry's resignation, she said, students had been organizing to put pressure on school officials and faculty to increase the number of minority professors and lecturers who would be given an opportunity to attain tenure and be recognized for their academic and professional achievements.

About 200 students turned out for the campuswide meeting which, among other things, prompted a proposal that an outside consultant be hired to review faculty hiring and promotion policies for conscious or unconscious bias and to recommend possible improvements.

"The words 'racism' and 'sexism' are such tension-ridden words these days, it's hard for people to confront more subtle biases that you grow up with," said Day. "We need the perspective of an outsider to see if there really is a commitment to meritocracy."

Brest said he was seriously considering the consultant idea. It is one of several proposals to be discussed at a series of meetings he has scheduled later this month with the faculty appointments committee and students, he said.

Mabry's experience was all too typical of the treatment of minorities by "relevant key faculty" at the law school, said longtime Stanford law professor William B. Gould, an African American and former chairman of the National Labor Relations Board.

"In many instances the competence of minorities is just not taken seriously," he said. "The fact of the matter is that this faculty is badly in need of education in race relations."

But he said Brest is the "best dean we've had in the 27 years I've been here."

***

Chronicle of Higher Education[8]
March 12, 1999

Stanford Law School Faces Tensions Over Issues of Race and Gender
By Katherine S. Mangan

For the first time in its history, Stanford Law School has appointed a woman as its new dean, and it couldn't have come at a better time.

The school has been battling accusations by some faculty members and students that it fosters a climate that is hostile toward women and members of minority groups -- a charge that law-school officials vehemently deny.

Kathleen M. Sullivan's appointment as dean, which is scheduled to take effect in September, is a milestone not only for the law school, but for the university. None of the university's colleges has ever been headed by a woman.

Ms. Sullivan, who could not be reached for comment, has been a professor of law at Stanford since 1993 and is considered one of the nation's top constitutional-law scholars. She will replace Paul Brest, who announced last year that he planned to step down after 12 years as dean.

At Stanford, a series of events has triggered accusations of racism and sexism. The most recent incident occurred last month when a law student sent an electronic message to his constitutional-law class, attacking a black visiting law professor. Students accused the anonymous sender of racism, and criticized Mr. Brest for failing to act forcefully enough to find and punish the student.

That incident came on the heels of the December resignation of Linda Mabry, one of five minority professors out of the law school's 40 faculty members.

Ms. Mabry, who was an associate professor when she resigned, was due to be considered for tenure in two years. She said she had no reason to think her tenure case was in jeopardy, and "had been given every indication that everything was on track." However, when she quit, effective last December, she said that a series of incidents had convinced her that the law school was a "hostile climate for women and people of color."

What finally triggered her resignation, she said, was learning that the law school was planning to open a new program in her area of expertise -- international-business law -- and hadn't consulted her. She said that oversight reflected a pattern, in which her male colleagues failed to take her scholarship or her contributions to the law school seriously. She said she first learned of the new program "when I read a flier inviting students to a

---

meeting." She added: "It was demoralizing and embarrassing to be excluded from the discussion. It was as if I were invisible."

Ms. Mabry is one of 15 current and former faculty members from across the university who have filed a complaint with the U.S. Department of Labor, alleging that Stanford's tenure and promotion practices are discriminatory. "We're simply asking to be treated equally, but we're held to a higher standard than our white, male colleagues," Ms. Mabry said. She is uncertain whether she will remain in academe or practice law.

All calls to the law school were referred to Dean Brest.

In an interview, he said he could not discuss the details of Ms. Mabry's case. However, in a speech last week to Stanford alumni in Washington he said only that her charges were "unfounded." In his speech, Mr. Brest said that Stanford has a greater proportion of black and Latino faculty members than any other top law school in the country.

Mr. Brest said the school was rethinking some of the ways it had gone about recruiting minority faculty members, such as hiring lawyers with limited experience in publishing scholarly articles. In retrospect, he said, such practices, have "not furthered the school's efforts to retain faculty of color. It has diverted some promising careers in law practice, and has also led to claims that Stanford has a 'revolving door' for minority faculty."

While Dean Brest did not refer specifically to Ms. Mabry as an example of that problem, much of her career has been spent in private practice or government service.

Ms. Mabry, however, said the recent e-mail incident reflected the same kind of racial bias she experienced. She called the target of the e-mail message, Kendall Thomas, "a superb teacher and scholar" who is held to a higher standard by some students because of his race.

In his e-mail message, the anonymous student referred to Mr. Thomas, a visiting professor from Columbia University, as a "sluggard" and a "windbag" and questioned his qualifications. The message resulted in a volley of heated e-mail exchanges between several students and the anonymous author, in which the author also attacked a student and another faculty member.

Some students criticized Mr. Brest for defending the sender's right to remain unidentified. The dean, in turn, has criticized students for resorting to "mob hysteria" and ignoring the student's constitutional rights. In an e-mail message to students, Mr. Brest condemned the content of the message, but said that its author's decision to remain anonymous was protected by the First Amendment.

Mr. Thomas did not return telephone calls, but he told the campus newspaper, The Stanford Daily, that the e-mail message and its aftermath had "much more to do with student life than with me."

In his own e-mail message last month, Dean Brest wrote that "anonymity was nothing but a cowardly shield behind which the author launched vicious attacks on a guest at our school, a current faculty member, and a classmate." In a subsequent e-mail message, the author apologized, saying the letter was not intended to be racist.

About 150 students met with the dean last month to discuss the incident. Some students complained that the administration hadn't gone far enough.

"This was an opportunity for the administration to make a strong stand against anonymous hate speech, but instead, it swept the matter under the rug," said Dominique Day, a third-year law student who is black. "This amounts to a quiet tolerance of bigotry in the law school."

In an interview, Mr. Brest expressed anger at the students' response. "For law students to be reckless about First Amendment rights and university rules is really appalling," he said. "They were just out for blood."

END notes

[i] Free University of Brussels

[ii] *Federal Aid Highway Act of 1956* – the largest public works project in American history to that point.

[iii] John F. Kennedy in his civil rights speech of June 11, 1963, asked for legislation "giving all Americans the right to be served in facilities which are open to the public—hotels, restaurants, theaters, retail stores, and similar establishments," as well as "greater protection for the right to vote." A few months later he was assassinated – 22 November, 1963.

[iv] **Andrew Goodman** (November 23, 1943 – June 21, 1964) was one of three American civil rights activists who were murdered near Philadelphia, Mississippi, during Freedom Summer in 1964 by members of the Ku Klux Klan. The Walden School, at 88th Street and Central Park West, named its middle and upper school building in Goodman's memory. Several films were based on their story, including Alan Parker's *Mississippi Burning*, 1989, and *Murder in Mississippi*, 1990.

[v] **Freedom Summer** (also known as the Mississippi Summer Project) was a campaign in the United States launched in June 1964 to attempt to register to vote as many African American voters as possible in Mississippi, which up to that time had almost totally excluded black voters. The project was organized by the Council of Federated Organizations (COFO), a coalition of four established civil rights organizations: the National Association for the Advancement of Colored People (NAACP), the Congress of Racial Equality (CORE), the Southern Christian Leadership Conference (SCLC) and the Student Nonviolent Coordinating Committee (SNCC), with SNCC playing the lead role.

[vi] 'Napoleon Rivers Born December 1, 1872 Died 1963"

[vii] Malcolm 'X' Little, El-Hajj Malik El-Shabazz was assassinated near Harlem, February 21, 1965 (aged 39).

[viii] **Rogers, J. A** *Sex and Race.* New York J. A. Rogers Publications. 1940, 302 p. Undermining the concept of Aryan purity, this title is one of several works by Rogers who sought to demonstrate the achievements of Black culture. It explores Blacks in early Japanese, Jewish, Greek and Roman culture as well as Black religious figures. An immigrant from Jamaica, he lived in Harlem and Chicago, and worked as a Pullman Porter. In the 1920s he became a journalist for the *Daily Negro Times*, and was the only Black war correspondent during World War II. *Sex and Race* is a

three volume set published from 1940 to 1944.

[ix] Located at Central Park West and 88th Street, the private **Walden School** was formed in 1914 by Margaret Naumburg, whose work influenced the nation's educational philosophy. The school stressed allowing students to develop their identities, in large measure through the visual and performing arts. For 73 years an innovator in progressive unconventional education, it closed in 1987 following a real-estate dispute. Graduates included Barbara Tuchman, the historian; Mike Nichols, the director; Carol Gilligan, the educational psychologist, and Matthew Broderick, the actor.

[x] **Miriam Makeba** (4 March 1932 - 9 November 2008) was a Grammy Award-winning South African singer.

[xixi] **Br'er Rabbit** is a picaresque character from the Uncle Remus stories of the American South. "Tar Baby" was originally a saga in American Cherokee Indian tradition, published in 1845. Joel Chandler Harris's popular editions date to the 1870s, later rewritten for children by Enid Blyton.

[xii] Four years before the riots Linda refers to, Time Magazine ran a front cover article about **Harlem** which provides some context for the Jewish shops being attacked:

Negro politicians stir passions when they point out that 80% of Harlem's businesses are owned by whites who do not live there. Most of them are Jews, and here are the sparks of Harlem's blazing anti-Semitism. The fact is that some of Harlem's most flourishing enterprises are run by black millionaires who don't live there either, but at least they are black. "If we are unable to bring about an orderly transfer of business from whites to Negroes in Harlem, it will be done one way or the other," thunders James Lawson, president of the United African Nationalist Movement, head of the Harlem Council for Economic Development and a thoroughgoing demagogue. What Lawson means is clear. Last April half a dozen Negro punks entered a husband-and-wife clothing store on 125th Street, got into an argument and stabbed the wife, Mrs. Magit Sugar, to death with a double-edged dirk. Lawson said that the store, once worth $5,000, could now be bought from disconsolate Frank Sugar, a Hungarian refugee, for $150. Similar "expropriations," he predicts, will take place if whites do not sell out to Negroes.

– *No Place Like Home*, Time Magazine, Friday, Jul. 31, 1964, no byline.

[xiii] **Mount Holyoke College** is a highly selective liberal arts women's college in South Hadley, Massachusetts. Originally founded by Mary Lyon as Mount Holyoke Female Seminary in 1837, it is the "first of the Seven Sisters" and is "the oldest continuing institution of higher education for women in the world."

[xiv] A "**Medicaid mill**" is a health clinic that scams Medicare/Medicaid by running up health costs. The term was popular in the early 1970s.

[xv] Dr. **Condoleezza Rice** served as the Secretary of State of the United States from Jan. 26, 2005 until Jan. 20, 2009. Between 1993 and 1999, Ms Rice was Stanford University's Provost, the institution's chief budget and academic officer. Born November 14, 1954 in Birmingham, Alabama, she earned her bachelor's degree in political science, *cum laude* and *Phi Beta Kappa*, from the University of Denver in 1974; her master's from the University of Notre Dame in 1975; and her Ph.D. from the Graduate School of International Studies at the University of Denver in 1981.

[xvi] Professor **Taylor- Thompson**, a graduate of Yale Law School, began her

teaching career at Stanford Law School where she was the recipient of the Outstanding Teaching Award from the Associated Students for the University. In 1994, she received the law school's John Hurlburt Award for Excellence in Teaching.

xvii **The New Yorker,** October 18, 1999, P.144 *Schools Are Her Business,* John Cassidy.

xviii **Caroline Minter Hoxby** is a labor and public economist whose research focuses on issues in education and local public economics. Currently, she is the Scott and Donya Bommer Professor in Economics at Stanford and director of the Economics of Education Program for the National Bureau of Economic Research. She is also a Senior Fellow of the Hoover Institution and the Stanford Institute for Economic Policy Research.

xix **Judith L. Swain,** M.D., a molecular cardiologist, is chair of the Department of Medicine at the Stanford University School of Medicine.

xx **Thomas C. Heller** became the Lewis Talbot & Nadine Hearn Shelton Professor of International Legal Studies in the Stanford Law School effective December 9, 1996.

(www.law.stanford.edu/display/images/dynamic/people_cv/heller_cv.pdf, Accessed June 4, 2009). Heller was hired directly into a tenured position in the Law School seventeen years earlier, in 1979.

xxi **A Deweyan Perspective on the Economic Theory of Democracy.** 11 CONSTITUTIONAL COMMENTARY 539 (1995).

xxii **Peggy Radin** is Professor of Law at Stanford University. Previously, she was Of Counsel at Heller Ehrman White & McAuliffe and Of Counsel at Fenwick & West, and Professor of Law at the University of Southern California.

xxiii **Professor Janet Halley** is the Royall Professor of Law at Harvard Law School. Previously, she was Professor of Law at Stanford Law School (1991-2000) and Assistant Professor of English at Hamilton College (1980-85). She has a Ph.D. in English from UCLA (1980) and a J.D. from Yale Law School (1988).

xxiv **Kenneth E. Scott** is the Ralph M. Parsons Professor of Law and Business, Emeritus, and a senior research fellow at the Hoover Institution.

xxv **Ian Ayres** wrote an op-ed piece his senior year called "Black Like Me," a controversial piece detailing his selection of the "African- American" box for race on his PSAT. He is the William K. Townsend Professor at the Yale Law School and is Professor at the Yale School of Management. Ayres has also taught the Stanford Law School, among other places.

xxvi **Nina Rachel Rosenhan,** 34, a 6-year resident of Palo Alto, died Oct. 2 [1996] in a car accident while visiting friends in England. A graduate of Gunn High School, she later attended the University of California at Santa Cruz and San Jose State University. She headed the financial department of Fast Multimedia in Foster City. Besides embroidering her own designs, she was also an avid gardener, photographer and chef. She worked on behalf of Bosnian refugees and supported the New Israel Fund and the Jewish Community Federation of San Francisco. She is survived by her parents, Mollie and David Rosenhan; a brother, Jonathan "Jack" Rosenhan; two sisters, Margaret Golden of Mountain View and Shelly Shick of San

Francisco. Services have been held. Contributions may be made to the New Israel Fund at 1853 Union St., San Francisco, CA 94123; the Children's Hospital at Stanford for the treatment of asthmatic children; Bosnian Relief; or a charity of the donor's choice. [PaloAltoOnline]

xxvii **David Rosenhan** is Professor Emeritus in a joint appointment with the Stanford University Department of Psychology.

xxviii **Lawrence B. Rabkin** is the chairman and managing director of law firm Howard Rice Nemerovski Canady Falk & Rabkin, where he concentrates on general corporate and business counseling, securities law, mergers and acquisitions and financial services regulation.

xxix **Howard, Rice, Nemerovski, Canady, Robertson, Falk & Rabkin** – eminent San Francisco law firm.

xxx **Barbara H. Fried** is the William W. and Gertrude H. Saunders Professor of Law at Stanford.

xxxi **Janet Cooper Alexander** is the Frederick I. Richman Professor of Law at Stanford.

xxxii **Barbara Babcock** was the first woman appointed to the regular faculty of the Stanford Law School, as well as the first woman to hold an endowed chair. As the Judge John Crown Professor of Law, Emerita, at Stanford, she is also the first emerita in the Law School.

xxxiii **Kathleen M. Sullivan** is a member of the Stanford Law School faculty and an elected fellow of the American Academy of Arts and Sciences.

xxxiv **Ellen Borgersen**, a former partner with Morrison & Foerster, was appointed an Associate Professor of Law at Stanford Law School in 1983, where she taught Civil Procedure and Complex Litigation and served as Associate Dean for Academic Affairs from 1989 to 1994. She returned to the firm as Of Counsel in 1998.

xxxv **Morrison & Foerster**, one of the nation's premier law firms, based in San Francisco, is known for its commitment to diversity.

xxxvi **Paul Heller** was hired directly into a tenured position in the Law School in 1979. Unlike Linda, he was never subjected to any tenure requirements. The publications section of the Stanford Law School website show that at the time he was given tenure he had published just two peer-reviewed journal articles in an academic career spanning eight years. One article came out in 1974, the other in 1976, and both were in the *Wisconsin Law Review,* a journal at the law school where he was employed from 1971 to 1977.

(www.law.stanford.edu/publications/search/?search=heller, accessed June 5, 2009). By the time of Linda's departure in 1999, it appears that Heller had added just two peer-reviewed journal articles to his publications, one in 1984 and one in 1996. In an academic career spanning almost three decades, most of it with tenure, Heller had produced only as much as was being required of Linda for tenure. Requests to Paul Heller for more information on his publication record have so far not produced a response.

xxxvii **Elspeth Farmer** was a visiting scholar at the Stanford Law School and the Institute for Research on Women and Gender during Linda time at Stanford. Her areas of research were comparative criminal law and sentencing. She was previously an assistant federal public defender and a visiting scholar in comparative criminal law in Germany.

xxxviii **Susan Liautaud** (Stanford '85, MA '86; Columbia Law School '89) was appointed Lecturer and Associate Dean for International and Graduate Programs in the Law School for the period 2000-02. She is married to Bernard Liautaud, co-founder in 1990 of Business Objects. They provided generous financial support to the 2001 Campaign for the Lucile Packard Children's Hospital at Stanford. We have been unable to find any record of academic publications for Ms. Liautaud.

xxxix **Paul Brest,** a former dean of Stanford Law School and a fellow in the American Academy of Arts and Sciences, assumed the presidency of the William and Flora Hewlett Foundation in 2000. Before joining the Stanford Law School faculty in 1969, he clerked for the U.S. Court of Appeals for the First Circuit and for the Supreme Court of the United States, and did civil rights litigation with the NAACP Legal Defense and Education Fund in Mississippi.

xl **Joseph A. Grundfest** joined the Stanford Law School faculty in 1990.

xli **Miguel A. Méndez.** After a litigation career in public interest law that included work for the Mexican American Legal Defense and Educational Fund and California Rural Legal Assistance, **Miguel A. Méndez** joined the Stanford Law School faculty in 1997.

xlii **Struggles in Steel: The Fight for Equal Opportunity** (1996)

xliii Editor's note.

xliv **Colleen E. Crangle** holds a Ph.D. from Stanford University (1984) in Logic, Philosophy of Language, and Philosophy of Science and Masters and a cum laude Bachelors degrees in mathematics and computer science from South African universities. Since leaving Stanford in 1997 she has been a principal in ConverSpeech LLC, Palo Alto, Visiting Professor in the School of Computing and Information Engineering at the University of Ulster, Northern Ireland, and the recipient of three research awards from the National Institutes of Health, continuing the research she had been doing at Stanford.

xlv **Edward H. Shortliffe** is now Professor of Biomedical Informatics at Arizona State University and of Basic Medical Sciences, University of Arizona College of Medicine – Phoenix.

xlvi At the end of 1998, seventeen women at Stanford compiled a report describing discrimination and retaliation practices at Stanford and submitted it to the Department of Labor. An investigation was launched shortly thereafter. As the recipient at that time of more than $500 million annually in federal contract payments and grants, Stanford University is obligated to abide by the requirements of Executive Order 11246, which prohibits discrimination on the basis of race, color, religion, sex, or national origin and mandates action to ensure equal opportunity. The regulations that implement Executive Order 11246 are enforced by the Department of Labor.

xlvii **Dr. Denise Johnson** became in 1989 the first African-American woman hired in the General Surgery Department. In her complaint to the Department of Labor she said she suffered steady harassment from her superiors and was ultimately fired from the Stanford-affiliated Palo Alto Veterans Administration Medical Center in 1997 because she refused to take part in firing or demoting two physicians at the medical center. Johnson's firing was especially painful because it came three months after her husband died in an auto accident. "We all feel ... they have decided to get rid of these strong women," said Johnson. "The university has chosen to use its vast resources and influence to wear us down."

[xlviii] **Jessica Agramonte** is an Assistant Professor - Medical Center Line – in the Department of Orthopaedic Surgery and the director of the Motion & Gait Analysis Lab at Lucile Packard Children's Hospital.

[xlix] **Lawrence M. Fagan** continues to function as co-director of the Program in Biomedical Informatics at Stanford.
[l] **Psalm 62**:1-2, New King James Version

[li] **William B. Gould IV** joined the Stanford Law School Faculty in 1972. Professor Gould's work includes his historical record of the experiences of his great-grandfather in Diary of a Contraband: The Civil War Passage of a Black Sailor, and his own Washington story, Labored Relations: Law, Politics and the NLRB: A Memoir.

[lii] **Hank Greely** joined the Stanford Law School Faculty in 1985.

[liii] **Children of the dream** In his "I have a dream" speech, Martin Luther King Jr. envisioned "his children living in a nation not judged by the color of their skin but by the content of their character."

[liv] **A Great Day In Harlem**. Art Kane, a freelance photographer working for Esquire magazine, took this picture. It was published in the January 1959 issue. Around 10 a.m. in the summer of 1958, 57 musicians gathered on 126th Street, between Fifth and Madison Avenues in Harlem. They included Count Basie, Art Blakey, Dizzy Gillespie, Coleman Hawkins, Charles Mingus, Thelonious Monk, Gerry Mulligan, Oscar Pettiford, Sonny Rollins and Lester Young.

[lv] **Marlbrough s'en va-t-en guerre** "Marlborough Has Left for the War" is one of the most popular folk songs in the French Language. This burlesque lament on the death of John Churchill, 1st Duke of Marlborough (1650–1722) was written on a false rumor of that event after the Battle of Malplaquet in 1709. It tells how Marlborough's wife, awaiting his return from battle, is given the news of her husband's death. The melody probably predates the song's words and has been adapted for English in the song "For He's a Jolly Good Fellow."

[lvi] **Marlbrough s'en va-t-en guerre** "Marlborough Has Left for the War" is one of the most popular folk songs in the French Language. This burlesque lament on the death of John Churchill, 1st Duke of Marlborough (1650–1722) was written on a false rumor of that event after the Battle of Malplaquet in 1709. It tells how Marlborough's wife, awaiting his return from battle, is given the news of her husband's death. The melody probably predates the song's words and has been adapted for English in the song "For He's a Jolly Good Fellow."

[lvii] Copyright 1999 **The Washington Post** September 18, 1999, Saturday, Final Edition OP-ED; Pg. A19; **Affirmative Inaction**

We were astonished to read Geneva Overholser's Sept. 7 op-ed piece hailing Condoleezza Rice as a woman who "shows deep concern for inequity." Overholser's disregard of Rice's record at Stanford University is shocking. During

174

Rice's tenure as provost, complaints of race and gender bias in hiring, promotion and allocation of research funds skyrocketed. In response to a 400-page complaint submitted by female and minority faculty, the Labor Department is investigating the university for widespread discrimination in violation of federal equal opportunity laws. At stake is the more than $ 500 million that Stanford receives annually in government contracts and grants. Overholser praises Rice's "powerful skepticism" for anything that "smacks of softness or lack of discipline when it comes to extending opportunity." In that same vein, Rice derides affirmative action as a "slippery slope" that allows the promotion of "borderline" women but not "borderline" men. In response to criticisms concerning the lack of diversity in the Stanford faculty, Rice said "I do not believe in, and in fact will not apply, affirmative action" in promotions. However, speaking of her own rise to power at Stanford, she proclaimed "I myself am a beneficiary of a Stanford strategy that took affirmative action seriously." By her own account, she was a "risk" when she was appointed to the faculty, and when later appointed provost, she lacked even the experience of chairing a department.

So are we to believe that affirmative action worked for her but would be "soft" and show a lack of "discipline" for everyone else? This contradiction is either stupid, dishonest or both. For reasons we cannot fathom, Rice is loath to extend to others the same considerations that lifted her to a position of power and privilege.

Linda Mabry and Colleen Crangle

Linda Mabry is a former associate professor at Stanford Law School and Colleen Crangle is a former senior research scientist at the Stanford School of Medicine.

[lviii] See *Gender Equity at Stanford University: One Woman's Story* in 'Sex discrimination in the workplace: multidisciplinary perspectives" (Eds.) Faye J. Crosby, Margaret S. Stockdale, S. Ann Ropp and *Gender equity - Dr Colleen Crangle's story* **as told to Gary Burd (Executive Editor) Biochemist** VOLUME 24 NO 2 April 2002.